THE BUDGET KIT

SIXTH EDITION

Other Books by the Author

The Money Tracker: A Quick and Easy Way to Keep Tabs on Your Spending

101 Great Ways to Improve Your Life, Volume 2 (contributing author)

The Family Memory Book: Highlights of Our Times Together

Magic, Miracles and Synchronicity: A Journal of Gratitude and Awareness
(formerly *Daily Riches: A Journal of Gratitude and Awareness*)

Common Cent$: The Complete Money Management Workbook
(forerunner to the current *Budget Kit*)

THE COMMON CENTS MONEY MANAGEMENT WORKBOOK

THE BUDGET KIT

SIXTH EDITION

JUDY LAWRENCE

KAPLAN

PUBLISHING

New York

© 1993, 1997, 2001, 2004, 2008, and 2011 by Judy Lawrence

Previously published as *Common Cent$: The Complete Money Management Workbook*

Author photo © Kim Jew Photography Studio

Published by Kaplan Publishing, a division of Kaplan, Inc.
395 Hudson Street
New York, NY 10014

Printed in the United States of America

10 9 8 7 6 5 4 3 2 1

ISBN 13: 978-1-60714-860-9

Kaplan Publishing books are available at special quantity discounts to use for sales promotions, employee premiums, or educational purposes. For more information or to purchase books, please call the Simon & Schuster special sales department at 866-506-1949.

Dedication

To my parents, who inspired my skills and interest in managing money and ultimately my financial career through their everyday examples

Contents

An inspirational story and practical suggestions for making
major life changes.

An overview of the variety of worksheets available for getting
the maximum benefit from this workbook. Also provides
insight for handling savings, electronic budgeting, and family
management of the budget.

Explore how the expanding world of cashless transactions
impacts your life. Learn how online and electronic money
management programs fit with your current system. *Find
resources and updates on credit reports and identity theft.*

A place to record online bill payment schedules, website
addresses, user IDs, passwords, password hints, and related
information.

PART ONE

A picture of your total financial worth. A valuable aid for loan
and insurance purposes.

A place to write your goals and a method to help you stay on
target for reaching those goals.

A reminder of items or services that each family member needs
and/or wants when extra money is available.

PART TWO

PART THREE

Preface

"My wife and I have used your book The Budget Kit *for several years now and have become quite good at controlling our income and expenses using this wonderful book—thanks to you! Your budgeting techniques have revolutionized our financial lives, and we are grateful to you, to say the least. I really do appreciate your influence on our financial lives. My three children will also appreciate your influence on our lives when they're able to go to college and have it completely paid for because their parents found you soon enough."*

—Andrew H., SC

We've all heard the saying "If it's not broke, don't fix it." That idea has certainly applied to this workbook, which has been around since 1981 when I originally self-published it as *Common Cent$*. Over the years, there have been minor revisions and additions to reflect the needs of the times.

Now, as this workbook continues in its fourth decade, a new millennium, a world of high-speed Internet answers to everything, and an economy struggling to recover from high unemployment and strained personal budgets, I am pleased to say that the core money-management concepts and worksheets provided in these pages are more timely and effective than ever. Even if you have transitioned to financial software and online banking, you will find the overall budgeting process, the organized layout, the concepts, and the comprehensive categories to be extremely helpful and transferable as you move to the electronic level of managing your finances. This information will also help you gain confidence and stay in financial control during this electronic transition.

Each revision, including this one, came as a result of many wonderful reader comments and suggestions, as well as my own seminar and one-on-one counseling experience with hundreds of clients over the years. While listening to the specific concerns, comments, and questions, I recognized a need for additional explanation of core budgeting concepts. With this edition, I have expanded the information on some of the core worksheets in Part Two. I continue to welcome your recommendations for enhancing this workbook so it best fits your needs and helps you reach your goals.

My intention always was and still is to help you get started by providing a guideline or road map that is flexible enough to accommodate the many unique regional and personal situations as well as software packages that exist. The variety of worksheets throughout this workbook are designed to give you an overall and meaningful view of your monthly and yearly finances at a glance. Modify them as needed to fit your particular needs and lifestyle.

With the recession of the last few years, you may now have a greater need than ever to modify these worksheets for your unique financial situation. Even if you are dealing with a reduced fixed income or a variable income, escalated debt, or a defaulted mortgage or if you are recovering from bankruptcy, the concepts and numerous adaptable worksheets are still exceptional tools to help guide you through this period.

One woman looking at this workbook at one of my seminars asked, "Where's the theory?" The "theory" can be found in almost every personal finance book on the market. I'll bet you have a few of those books on your eReaders or bookshelves right now. Most of these books discuss volumes of valuable financial information. For a list of helpful books and resources, see the **Recommended Reading** and **Online Resources** sections in the back of this book. The authors usually encourage readers to establish a budget or spending plan and briefly discuss and show some examples. That still leaves the actual "doing it" part up to you, and that's usually where the procrastination, confusion, or fear sets in.

If you haven't been taught how to manage money and set up a budget, how would you know what to do? Just having money does not necessarily guarantee your ability to manage it. Not everyone has the time, knowledge, or organizational skills to set up a simple, functional system for managing all their daily, monthly, and yearly finances. That's why I designed and wrote this down-to-earth, realistic workbook. Instead of theory, the *focus of this workbook is to complement the other financial books and give you a tool you can pick up, quickly read, and easily and confidently start to use at any time by just gathering your financial papers, pencil, calculator, and eraser or by opening your favorite spreadsheet or personal finance software.*

As a counselor, I originally designed this workbook for young families and for women who were suddenly widowed or divorced, had limited money-management skills, and who often were intimidated by the whole idea of dealing with money. I soon realized, through my seminars, clients, and from the many letters and phone calls I received from people of all professions and incomes, that managing finances is a universal concern.

In fact, don't feel you are alone if managing your finances during these times as an individual or a couple is feeling like a real challenge. Even though our technology and education has become more sophisticated, more and more of my clients are professional attorneys, accountants, bank VPs, coaches, business owners, and more. All are trying to weave their way through the endless financial and personal responsibilities and challenges of today's fast paced and demanding lifestyles and weakened economy and still find peace and clarity in the process.

I also saw consumer debt remain a major universal concern over the decades. What an irony this was during the prosperous, boom times of the late 1990s and early 2000s. We were witnessing some of the lowest unemployment numbers, greatest economic growth, and highest investment returns this country had ever experienced, yet debt continued to hit all-time highs instead of going down.

Now, after the economic meltdown of 2008–2009, as more people deal with foreclosures and bankruptcies, the need for effectively managing personal finances and personal debt is stronger than ever. The **Debt Payoff Record** section of this workbook is designed to help you manage your debt and motivate you to get out of debt. *Through this worksheet, you can see at a glance your successful progress toward financial independence and financial control as you pay down, and ultimately pay off, your debt.*

Once you take the time to start organizing and planning your financial affairs with these worksheets, the results will be extremely rewarding. Remember, this workbook is a tool for you to use. By itself, it will not change anything. *With your input and your consistent and thorough participation in setting your goals, planning your expenses, recording and paying attention to your spending, and utilizing the many valuable sections, this workbook will help you create magic with your finances.*

The magic will be in the form of financial peace of mind replacing financial chaos. Bill paying will be more manageable and automatic, which alone will save hundreds of dollars from late-fee expenses. Getting into the savings habit will be easier and more rewarding as you use the different savings records and watch your balances grow. Tax time will flow more smoothly when you use the tax-deduction records and have all the information you need at your fingertips. Keeping child support records will be more effective with the guiding worksheets. These records could provide that extra edge or make the deciding difference if you ever need to go back to court and verify any information.

And, finally, life will take on a whole new meaning when your stress level around money is greatly reduced and at last there is room for those other aspects of your life to come back into focus and balance.

Over the years, many of my readers have told me about the new sense of balance and control they were able to achieve by using this workbook. It has been extremely gratifying for me to learn how readers were able to purchase their first home, save their marriage, get out of debt, and start saving and investing money for the first time. Using this workbook has literally changed lives. I look forward to hearing how it changes yours. One reader even calls this workbook "Frank." See the delightful story below. I wish you a successful and prosperous year.

"I think the worksheets are very useful. A lot of people can conceptualize how to budget and what they need to do, but it can be another story to actually put all that down on paper and make it

work…Somewhere within the process of getting my finances under control, I decided I wanted to give my budget a name. Not calling it something like "My Budget" exactly, but giving it a human name. As silly and ridiculous as it sounds, it actually helped a lot I think. I decided to name him "Frank," because I had to be frank with myself about my spending. I had to quit lying to myself about spending, and had to honestly make big changes. It was also easier for me, because rather than moaning and groaning about my stupid budget and how much I hated it and blah blah blah, I could just say that I had Frank keeping me in check. In Frank's journal, I purposely became emotional about him. I have entries where I tell Frank that I hate him, that he upsets me, and that I don't like having to have him. In other entries, I tell Frank that I'm so glad I have him because I'm happier, less stressed, and feel more under control."

—Kerri H., IA

Prologue

As I finished the 2001 revision of *The Budget Kit* and prepared to mail it to the publisher, a very special friend stopped me and said the book was not yet complete. She told me I needed to share my story of how I recently made a major mental, emotional, and geographical shift in my life and ultimately landed in my own paradise. After some consideration, I agreed.

My goal for my readers and clients always has been to uplift, encourage, and instill hope and confidence. From the response I received to this first prologue, I knew I had touched a special chord for people. I hope the following story will inspire you to make whatever changes in your life you feel you need to make to step into your own dreams.

Going from the Desert to the Valley

Sometimes when things just don't seem to flow, and more and more of life seems like a struggle, I have learned it is time to stop and reflect. That time had come for me by the late 90s. Living in Albuquerque, New Mexico, was always a wonderful experience. The climate, uniqueness, and beauty of the land, fulfilling friendships, and my professional budget counseling practice all were very satisfying to me. I never thought that I would someday want to leave or—more precisely—*have to* leave to really begin to thrive and move way beyond just surviving physically, emotionally, and financially.

I slowly began to realize that having loving friends, incredible respect in the professional community, and amazing hikes statewide somehow were not filling me up. As one wise woman recently put it, I was continually on simmer in life, but never getting to the rolling boil. I had lived in the desert—and a beautiful desert—for more than 20 years and started to feel like I had taken the desert into my cells. Having grown up in the green lands and blue lakes of Wisconsin, I realized my whole being was starving for the lushness of green and water again—as well as the lushness of creativity, innovation, and passion.

Somehow much of my life had taken on the aspects of the desert. My clients came to me with issues of lack. As much as I loved working with them (and know I have impacted their lives in a tremendously positive way), it was becoming apparent that I was continually being around the concept of lack in my work life. As I hiked the foothills of the Sandia Mountains every morning, I took in the real physical lack that is represented by the desert landscape. When there is not a lot of moisture, plants learn to hang on to what little rain they get and adapt the best way they can. That means their branches, stems, and leaves all have a stiffness, starkness, and brittleness to them as they conserve what little moisture they have to stay alive.

I was seeing this same analogy in my professional world. My clients, with limited funds and limited options for bringing in more money (New Mexico had been ranked 48 in per capita income for many years), found the most effective strategy for their families was to hang on, cut back, and conserve whatever way they could. As practical as that approach is, and as often as we have been taught the technique of "spend less or earn more" from all directions, I believe there are times and places when the toll of that approach is too high. You soon start to believe that life is only like a desert and start to forget that many other landscapes exist. And even when you start to realize that other landscapes do exist, the thought of what it would take to get there can be way too overwhelming or scary. So you live life on a continual low simmer and never really get to that boil stage of abundance, opportunity, choices, and vitality.

Change—Terror or Liberation?

Getting to that other stage would require change. Change, for the majority of us, is extremely challenging and frightening. And so, once again, staying with the familiar continues to have more appeal. That is, until the familiar becomes more uncomfortable and unbearable than the fear of the unknown.

I had reached that point. For three years I knew, on some level, I needed to make major changes in my life. And I resisted. So many things I tried just never fully panned out. Gregg Levoy, in his book *Callings: Finding and Following an Authentic Life,* talks about those callings, or messages. He tells stories of people taking up to five years before paying attention to what they needed to hear. That was helpful for me to know.

My turning point came when I woke up at 3 A.M. in a Chicago hotel in a panic attack. What was I going to do? The savings were going down even though I was a master at managing my money. The industry I was in was dramatically changing. There was no dependable, steady money coming in. The big chunks immediately got stashed for the lean times. I never felt I could really plan ahead. There was not a partner in my life to help support me emotionally, physically, or financially. I was not getting younger, even though I was blessed with good genes and excellent health.

> *"You do not get out of a problem by using the same consciousness that got you into it."*
>
> —Albert Einstein

How often I had heard the popular 12-step definition of insanity—doing the same thing over and over and expecting different results. I knew I was living my life in the same place, basically the same way, with a few attempted changes, and wanting different results—a different life. I knew I had to change my life, but how? I was afraid to loosen the grip on any money I did have out of fear of not having any more coming in. At 3 A.M. there was no one to call as I sat in that dark hotel room in total despair.

Then the answer started to formulate. Guidance was coming through. I had a check coming to me that week and I knew I had to use that money to propel me in my new direction as soon as possible. The money would not be used for one more month of mortgage and the usual bills, as that would only keep the same old pattern in place. I had been thinking about moving to the Silicon Valley in California after a friend had planted the seed in my mind two years earlier telling me stories about the start-ups and stock options. Words I didn't even understand. I knew then I had to go there and immerse myself in the middle of that energy of abundance.

The planning began for taking a quick trip. I had a friend there I knew would help me out, but what about the expense of the rental car, flight, and meals? The next day I called that friend, Carol, who graciously extended her home to me for three weeks. By the end of that day, she called me to say her friends wanted me to house-sit their beautiful home while they were on vacation and to feel free to use their car. The magical flow had begun. I always knew to trust when everything starts to fall into place easily. Next I called the Career Action Center and offered to volunteer for three weeks. I knew I needed to live as if I was living there and having a place to go every day. I now had a plan.

Welcome to the Valley

Two weeks later, I was in Cupertino, California, the home of Apple Computer. It didn't take me long to realize I had just gone from Sleepy Hollow to the Epicenter of the Galaxy. I had arrived at the height of the dot-com boom. The energy was off the charts. The traffic jammed. The housing and rental prices were too outrageous to even begin to think about. And still, I knew I had found my home. This was where I belonged.

Whatever it took, I knew I had to make the move. I had to totally change my life. It didn't matter that my computer skills were very limited. It didn't matter that my knowledge of technology was even more limited. Like a moth zooming to the light, I was choosing to head to the mother lode of computers and technology. If someone had told me I would move to Silicon Valley someday, I know I would have thought they were crazy. No way. Why move to the heart of the rat race? Yet there I was. I returned to Albuquerque and immediately put my condo up for sale in a market that was losing money. Next, I started going through stuff. It was time to clear out and move out!

Letting Go

I realized I couldn't get a *new* life if I kept holding on to all my *old* stuff. When planes are overweight with cargo, they can't take off from the runway and fly to the next destination. They need to clear out some baggage. And so I cleared 20 years of files and piles, drawers, closets, bookshelves, rooms, and my office. I let go of old patterns of hanging on to everything (whether for future use or recycling), attitudes that no longer served me, meetings and organizations that were no longer a fit for me. I got rid of furniture, appliances, my bed, and even my car. Time to buy a different car. The furniture and appliances could all be replaced. I had let go of my attachment to things. By the time I did move out in the fall of 1999, I left behind one very small but full storage shed, a few things at friends' homes, and took with me whatever could fit in my car.

That was not all that I took with me. Most important, I knew I was taking the essence of who I was. And that was the most valuable asset of all.

So what did I finally do about that outrageous housing market? I knew if I went down that path, I would be so terrified of the prices I would never leave my bed. Instead I decided to be financially creative. I put the word out everywhere before and after I moved that I would house-sit. Over four months I managed to house-sit in a variety of places in between staying with my friend Carol. By the last house-sitting arrangement, not only was I living rent free in a beautiful home with a pool once again, but I was getting paid well to feed Toots, the cat.

"What the mind can believe and conceive it can achieve."

—William James

Thinking Outside the Box Brings Dividends

So what was the key for me? During that whole process of knowing I needed to change right through to the point when I was determined to leave, I walked every morning along the foothills watching in my mind the video of the life I wanted to have. In my visionary world, the environment was sunny, lush, green, and fragrant. My workday consisted of doing satisfying work, making great money, and being part of a team of delightful, supportive, fun, bright, creative coworkers. People in general had an attitude of cooperation, appreciation, acceptance, diversity, creativity, potential, possibility, and vitality. The vision also included weekends of feeling the spray of the warm water as I slalom skied and enjoying the taste of the exquisite flavor of the salmon or trout on the houseboat trip. My energy level was high and sustained. I was happy, laughing a lot, thoroughly enjoying every experience and in total daily gratitude. In my core, I knew I was in total alignment and balance in my life.

To support this vision, I paid attention to all the signs around me whether from conversations, movies, books, birds, sounds, or even license plates. My journal is full of entries of one unbelievable synchronistic event after another.

My condo sold to a perfect buyer. Money kept coming from unexpected sources. Offers for storing or buying my things conveniently came to me. Everything flowed once I had made a clear decision to move.

Now, years later as I look back at this experience, I realize the true depth of this shift I had gone through as I processed those many lessons of life. Not only had I cleared out the external material clutter, but more significantly, the internal mental and emotional clutter. Once I was in this clear space, I was able to tap into my true authentic self, balance my head with my heart, and trust the results that would come.

This also explains more clearly why everything flowed once I had made that decision to move. Being in a clear inner space was the critical first step as I started creating the vision and the feeling of the life I really desired during those morning foothill walks.

When I originally wrote this story, I had lived in the Silicon Valley for only seven months. I absolutely loved it and was living most of my vision. I was a total match to the people and the creativity that surrounded me. The learning curve was extremely steep. As a very nontechnical person, I still managed to start working at an Internet start-up company. I finally understood and appreciated the term *lifelong learning*. I was pedalling as fast as I could to get up to speed with computers, the Internet, and technology in general. Through it all, I was blessed with patient, supportive people all around me who continually guided me through the next new learning speed bump.

Home at Last

Now, looking back ten years later, I appreciate having lived in the heart of Silicon Valley during the boom times as well as the dot-com crash, the real estate bubble and bust, full employment and then record unemployment, and finally the financial meltdown in California. During those years, I experienced my own financial roller coaster. Yet I can honestly still say it was the best move I ever made, and I will forever be grateful for all my wonderful experiences there and for all the truly remarkable people I came to know and love. Through it all, I was surrounded by an abundance of loving friends, cooperation, appreciation, diversity, creativity, innovation, and possibility. My nephew Dan once said, "Come to California, and you will find what you are looking for." He was right. I did and I will always cherish that phase of my life journey.

Even though I thought California would be my long-term home, it wasn't. At the peak of the recession, it became increasingly clear it was time for a major life change once again. The day came when I knew it was time to take up my generous friends on their loving offer to return to Albuquerque and stay with them for a while—at least until my California home sold. Year after year, they had been asking me to return to Albuquerque, but the timing just had not felt right. But by June of 2009, I was adjusting to a wonderful new life in Albuquerque, New Mexico.

I was back in the desert; only the desert felt different this time. At my bittersweet going-away ceremony in California, my friend Paula reminded me to look at my upcoming move as going *to* New Mexico, not *back* to New Mexico. That simple and subtle shift of perspective was powerful and enabled me to change the way I viewed and approached the move.

I discovered many changes, including an Albuquerque that was no longer feeling like Sleepy Hollow. This was a vibrant environment with many growing industries, including high-tech and green technology. Instead of only reconnecting with wonderful old friends in Albuquerque, I found myself utilizing my Silicon Valley networking skills to meet many fascinating, delightful new people. I enjoyed the gradual blending of my familiar friends and previous professional contacts with the new connections. Opportunities opened up. Members of the relatively new Albuquerque Collaborative Practice Group remembered my financial counseling work from earlier years and embraced both me and my counseling service. Ultimately the best part was the weaving of the new and the old and viewing it all with new eyes.

Over the years, I have learned to trust in divine timing. I learned a lot about myself during my California years and realized I actually love change. So my life journey continues from Albuquerque—the place I now call home.

A Financial Plan of Action for Change

I now encourage you to trust your own inner knowing. May my story or the following seven suggestions help you as you take your next step toward making a major change in life:

1. Find the balance between letting go and holding on. Letting go can mean relaxing your grip on your money, material possessions, ideas, or attitudes. It may mean a newfound sense of generosity or desire for service. Finding that balance means learning how to discern when it feels better to finally let go or when it feels more appropriate to hold on to your money, possessions, or behavior patterns and respectfully manage what you do have.

2. Create a vision of what you want. Dr. Fred Waddell uses his "miracle question." If you were to wake up tomorrow and, by some miracle, your life was everything you ever wanted, what would it be like? How would it look, feel, sound, smell, and be? How would you live your life? Who would be in your life? What would you change? What would stay the same? Dream up your magical scenario and write it down.

3. Find a moment every day to spend time with your vision. Nothing new here. I'm sure you have taken the classes and read the books on creating visions and making goals a reality. This time how will you actually do that? A daily walk, morning meditation, regular journaling? How will you incorporate the different senses as you step into this vision every day?

4. Start letting go of the "stuff." Clear the clutter in your life. Donate, give to others, have yard sales, toss. Do whatever it takes to start shifting the energy and begin the process of change.

5. Explore new experiences. Take new classes, meet new people, try new hobbies, sports, crafts, books, CDs, websites. Change your routine. Expand your life.

6. Move. Sometimes our lives can take on a whole new perspective by geographically being someplace new. Move to a new home or a different part of the town, your state, or even the country. Travel to different places. I read an article about the importance of a "latitude adjustment." Geography really does affect many people. I know that is why foreign travel always feels good for me.

7. Use the tools and techniques in this workbook to build your savings. Using practical tools is one way to stay grounded and take personal responsibility for your life. Having savings provides security, freedom, and choices. As one friend put it, "When I have 'drop dead' money in savings, I have the freedom to leave any job any time without having to compromise my integrity." Following the guidelines in this workbook will help you create that freedom and ability to step forward into your vision.

May you too find the right time and the right guidance for creating and attaining whatever changes you desire in your life.

Many blessings,
Judy Lawrence

Introduction
How to Use *The Budget Kit*

"This workbook took some of the fear out of money for me. By setting up an amount I knew I could spend in an area, I didn't feel so bad when I was spending that money. I knew it was planned and okay. Before, I was always in fear or guilt over everything I spent, thinking I was overspending."

The Purpose of This Workbook

The Budget Kit is designed to be easy to understand and practical to use. In today's environment, where a whole new population is endowed with a new-found sense of thrift and overall mindfulness about spending, this ease and practicality is once again timely and critical. Because this workbook is flexible, it can be used immediately regardless of the time of year or the condition of your finances. This is as true whether you receive a regular income from your job; fixed income from the government; or variable income from sales, contract work, investments, and other sources. By following the guidelines in this workbook, you will learn to take charge of your overall finances by anticipating your monthly and yearly expenses, instead of always reacting to crisis after crisis.

There are two purposes for this workbook. The first is to *help you keep proper records and get your financial information organized*. With this workbook, you can keep records of your daily, monthly, and yearly payments and expenses, medical costs, installment payments, credit card charges, mail order and online purchases, child support payments, savings, investments, retirement income, and much more.

The second purpose is to *help you successfully plan and manage your finances*. You can list and plan your goals; work out an estimating method for paying yourself (savings), your bills, and your monthly expenses; remind yourself of items you need or want to buy when extra money is available; and plan ahead for the periodic, but anticipated, expenses throughout the year.

You will probably notice the brief discussion on many of the financial topics mentioned throughout this workbook. This brevity was deliberate so the primary focus could remain on moving forward with action steps using the worksheets. There are already volumes of books and websites available for more in-depth information of each financial topic.

> **Please note:** *The concepts, information, and worksheets presented in this workbook are designed to apply to the majority of financial situations. This includes those unique changing economic events such as being laid off, living temporarily on unemployment, dealing with a reduced salary, going through a bankruptcy, adjusting to becoming a solo-preneur, as well as operating on a very fixed and limited income. In fact, the concepts presented here are almost more critical during those times than when you feel secure with a steady, stable income.*

How to Get Started

Set aside a block of time so you can thoroughly review the variety of sections available in this workbook. These sections contain instructions along with worksheets that were designed to address many different needs. Each worksheet can be used independently, with another, or as a setup guideline to use with any software you are using. Determine your own needs and see how this workbook will best fit them.

The many helpful worksheets in *The Budget Kit* are divided into three parts.

Part One helps you focus on *where you are and where you want to be* financially. Your *initial* time involved may be greater here as you gather and fill in the information. After completing this step, these pages become more of a place to revisit for reviewing and reflecting as the year goes on.

If this section feels a little overwhelming at this time, or you are very anxious to get started and want to jump right in and set up a spending plan, then move on to Part Two. Take a moment to skim through this first section and then come back later and complete it when it feels right for you.

Part Two is your action section *where you plan, project, and record on a daily, monthly, and yearly basis.* The bulk of your time and attention throughout the year will be spent in Part Two. You will quickly see how to anticipate those "unexpected" bills throughout the year, know how to plan out each month in advance, and learn where all your money is going.

All of this information and the way it is organized will be just as valuable if you are managing your finances electronically.

Part Three is a collection of a *variety of record-keeping worksheets for accommodating different individual needs.* This is where you can keep records concerning child support income, mail orders, subscriptions, investments, retirement, savings, and other miscellaneous information. You can also record such expenses as medical and dental (including insurance reimbursements) as well as tax deductions.

Take some time to look through all three parts and the worksheets in each part, and see which ones will be more helpful for your particular financial situation.

"Being recently divorced and new to managing money, I was surprised to find that using these worksheets actually energizes me! When I write everything down and have a plan, I find I am no longer worrying about it. It really makes a difference!"

Prepare for the Known, the Unknown, and your Dreams

By setting up your system for the year, you are planning ahead and getting a full financial picture. It won't be long before you see that you will need to have some system for saving money ahead of time for different purposes. Listed below are three different areas of savings I recommend you have.

1. Reserve account (the *known* expenses). After listing your major anticipated periodic or nonmonthly expenses throughout the year on your **Yearly Budget Worksheet** in Part Two (such as car insurance, home improvement plans, tuition, gifts, etc.), total these up. See the sample on page 53.

Divide this total number by 12 to calculate the monthly amount you need to set aside in a bank, credit union, or money market account for a reserve account. *Remember, this is not your emergency money. This is a savings for bills or expenses that will be coming due, but at various times of the year.*

By setting this money aside each month, you will feel like you magically have extra money available when some of the bigger expenses (such as a family vacation, property taxes, or graduation) come due. These infrequent expenses no longer will disrupt your whole monthly budget or land on your credit card.

Enter this reserve savings category and the amount on your **Monthly Budget Worksheet** in Part Two under "Fixed Amounts" at the top part of the page. (See page 69 for a sample.) Consider this part of "paying yourself first" as one of the fixed bills you pay each month.

"I just wanted to let you know how much your book changed the way I look at our money. In particular, the Yearly Budget made a HUGE impact on my thinking. It is amazing how much the yearly expenses can increase your overall expenses. Planning these expenses out in advance makes such a difference."

—Jennifer M., FL

2. Emergency account (the *unknown* expenses). There are going to be times when unknown disasters occur that create emergencies. Some examples are when the car breaks down, the home heating system needs to be replaced, your job position is eliminated, or your dental bridgework breaks.

The best way to have some peace of mind through any of these events is to know you have funds set aside in case an emergency occurs. Historically, the guideline has been to have three to six months' worth of take-home pay available. During these recent unstable recessionary times, however, new guidelines of eight to ten months have been recommended. Save this money in a bank, credit union, money market account, or mutual fund with check writing privileges.

Determine what amount you can realistically save each month (you may want to use payroll deductions), and slowly build this account up. Enter this monthly saved amount under "Fixed Amounts" on the **Monthly Budget Worksheet** in Part Two. (Again, see the sample on page 69.)

Remember this saved money in your emergency account for unexpected expenses and events is *not* to be confused with the reserve account, which actually is being saved for expenses that you know will occur.

3. Goals account (your *dream* account). An entire section in Part One is devoted to identifying goals and saving for them. This is the third amount that will be included under the "Savings" category in the "Fixed Amounts" section on the **Monthly Budget Worksheet** in Part Two. Initially, this number may be a much smaller amount or even nonexistent until the other two accounts get started and have sufficient funds available.

By including your reserve, emergency, and goals accounts on the **Monthly Budget Worksheet**, you have a way of putting together and seeing your total spending plan. *This process also reminds and encourages you to save and put funds aside regularly, offering you a system for staying aware and in control of your finances.*

Getting a Handle on Savings

If saving money is new for you, or has been difficult in the past, remember the most important part of this process is *starting.* If you can only start with $10 to $20 per pay period or per month in the beginning, that's okay. Start with that amount. Use automatic payroll deductions to make this habit easier for you. The significance of this monthly step is that you are establishing a very critical habit as well as starting to accumulate some savings. Don't be discouraged with the small amount in the beginning. When you keep up the saving habit, the balance in your savings will gradually grow. As you develop a more effective budget, the specific amount you are able to save each month will also start to grow.

Learning to plan and act proactively for the future will also serve you well the next time you receive a bonus, settlement, refund, or other lump sum of money. You will have more tools to discern how to utilize that money so it truly aligns with your overall goals and priorities, instead of just spending it mindlessly and spontaneously.

Remember to be realistic about the amount you can actually save in the beginning. Saving a small amount each month and leaving it in savings is much more productive financially and psychologically than depositing large amounts only to have to take money back out of savings each month to cover expenses. I have seen numerous clients with failed savings attempts and eroded confidence levels due to ambitious savings intentions, but with no backup spending game plan. Every time these clients withdrew money from their savings for basic living expenses, they were sabotaging themselves by subconsciously confirming their belief that they really can't save money. Once these clients developed a budget using many of the sections in this workbook, their savings plans stayed intact and grew in value. So did their confidence levels. One couple depends on the routine of planning meetings to keep their household of five flowing smoothly.

> *"Every Sunday night when the kids are in bed, we sit down and talk about the finances. We make decisions about expenses and decide if we should spend money on something or save it."*

Who Manages the Family Budget?

Who handles the finances in your household? Often one partner assumes and maintains the role of "family budget director." Many couples fall into their respective roles because they are good at it, like it, or have more time, or by default when one spouse refuses. These roles can often be logical and efficient provided that the family budget director is good at managing money. However, using this approach is not always the most effective in the long run, and once this pattern is set, it can last for years. Often it is an event that causes the routine to change.

I highly recommend that each spouse regularly be involved with the household finances in some way, even if that means trading off partial or full-time responsibility every six months, every year, or every other year. By getting involved with your household finances on some regular basis, you develop an awareness of your financial obligations, limitations, spending patterns, and overall current financial status. You also have a better appreciation of how expenses are going up—especially if you have a very active, athletic (and hungry) teenager. For example, the rising price of groceries and kids' shoes becomes very apparent.

This awareness is especially important for personal relationships. There may be times when occasionally the partner managing the finances must announce: "No, we can't afford that item or luxury right now." That news can easily conjure up a whole gamut of reactions for the uninvolved partner. Feelings of confusion and misunderstanding can translate into: "What do you mean? We were just paid three days ago. What are you doing with all the money?!"

If that person who blew up had firsthand experience with the bills and budget for the past six months, it would be easier to see the reason for the decision to cut back. It is difficult to know what you really can and cannot afford each month when you start losing that total sense of what it costs to run your household. You may not be as in touch with how school functions and last-minute events seem to gobble up the discretionary cash, how new digital equipment, monthly fees, and electronic games and devices tend to get more involved and more expensive, or how household repairs just manage to keep on piling up.

This mutual awareness by both partners is especially important if the designated Family Budget Director is suddenly in an accident or dealing with a long-term incapacitating illness in the hospital or suddenly dies or leaves due to a divorce. If the other partner is already familiar with the financial picture and the location of all the papers and records, then the trauma of the loss will not be compounded by the fear of taking on the new, often terrifying responsibility of handling all the finances.

Even without the traumatic circumstances, I have found many partners who confide that carrying this responsibility of having to make all the financial decisions alone for many years becomes a major emotional burden. Many times both partners are very relieved when I suggest that the responsibility be shared.

I strongly encourage couples to work together or trade off the responsibility of paying the bills and keeping records. Decide what works best for your situation and then follow through on that decision.

Family Affair

Financial discussions are also important to share with the whole family. Remember, you are being the financial role model for your children. You can do this deliberately or by default. One way to look at this is to ask yourself: "If my children were now adults and handling their money pretty much the way I do right now, would I be proud of how they were doing?" This question is more about a reality check and less about self-judgment.

Once you include the children in the decision process, you will be amazed at what insights they have to offer and how willing they are to cooperate.

If you are wondering how to get started, think of your family as a small business and consider having a weekly "family financial board meeting" on a regular fixed schedule. Set up the ground rules so everyone knows this is a safe and supportive place and time to express their thoughts and questions. It is a time for them to know they will be heard, not interrupted or put down. Establish an agenda where you will do your planning for the next week.

The following ideas are suggestions for how to productively use this family meeting time:

- Review your goals.
- Outline your spending choices and decisions.

- Determine charitable giving.
- Find creative ways to resolve money shortages or to utilize extra funds.
- Work out logistics of who will handle certain responsibilities.
- Be sure to acknowledge all the progress you have made as a team so far.

After a few months, or even weeks, you will begin to notice subtle changes everywhere—not just with the finances. Notice the shift in the family relationships, how the household is running, and the status of your checkbook balance.

> *"There were unexpected benefits from my new financial awareness. My relationships with my children improved as I set more honest boundaries that were truly appropriate for me. I got healthier physically, and I learned to do household things that I'd previously been afraid of, such as snow blowing and mowing my lawn."*
>
> —Char B., MI

Using *The Budget Kit* When Budgeting Electronically

You may be wondering how this workbook, with its manual fill-in-the-blank worksheets, fits in with today's convenient financial software or online programs.

One consistent theme I hear from readers around the world, who have selected *The Budget Kit* over hundreds of other books and programs, is how much they appreciate the "organic" way the worksheets are laid out and the commonsense approach and explanations used throughout. This is one of those "If it isn't broke, don't fix it" factors that keeps *The Budget Kit* timeless and useful in all economic situations.

As people have been transitioning from paper to digital, especially over the last ten years, I've noticed two interesting patterns. First, I've started hearing from more folks who used to manage their budgets successfully on paper and then switched to popular financial software programs. They would tell me that something had changed or been lost in the process, but they couldn't put their finger on what that change was. It seemed as though the planning, inputting, and visual awareness pieces had changed or been lost somehow. In their place were reams (or screens) of reports and averages, *yet people did not feel they had answers or clarity.*

The second pattern I noticed was that people who had created budgets for the first time by using popular software or online programs were experiencing limited success.

First of all, I do want to applaud people for being motivated and getting started—no matter what method they use.

In both cases, people are basically tracking their spending, which is a great start. Yet at the same time, they often don't have a full grasp of the concept of a comprehensive personal budget and, therefore, do not clearly know what they can and cannot manage each month. *Nor do they easily know approximately what periodic or unusual expenses to anticipate throughout the year or have a plan for handling any of those expenses.*

Consequently, they are not getting all of the benefits or information that they could from the process or tools they are using. In the meantime, *they are entering figures and seeing reports yet are not truly learning or understanding effective budgeting skills or concepts or even creating a realistic budget.* I often find that new clients, who are using popular software programs, have lots of information regarding their averages but can't figure out why their spending plans (budgets) are not working for them.

This is where *The Budget Kit* fits in. Even if you decide to use only a few of the hard-copy worksheets, or none of the worksheets, you will gain tremendous insight from reading and studying this workbook. By reading and understanding the overall core concepts I discuss and then reviewing how the worksheets are set up and explained, you will see how the smaller monthly and day-to-day pictures fit into the larger yearly picture. You will then have a more solid understanding of how to create and maintain a complete budget that factors in all the various financial pieces of your personal life and household. Armed with this better understanding, you can then utilize the powerful capabilities of any program and customize it to work for you by following the format or concepts gained from *The Budget Kit*.

When it Pays to Budget Manually

At the same time, if you are completely new to budgeting (no matter what your age) or have not been successful with budgets in the past, I would still suggest that you consider starting out manually with the worksheets in *The Budget Kit* for the first month or two instead of jumping into some digital program. You will become more familiar and comfortable with the natural layout of the worksheets and the down-to-earth concepts they incorporate. This will strengthen your ability to transfer your newly acquired information and skill level to any software.

Let me explain what I have observed over the last 30 years that I feel accounts for much of the success people have experienced using *The Budget Kit*. There is something very powerful about multisensory learning. Using *The Budget Kit* manually incorporates this learning in a more effective way than do electronic programs. Many of my readers recognized their overall financial situation very quickly and clearly as they *physically* wrote down the expenses on the worksheets. They *visually* took in those new expense numbers when added to the accumulated previous expenses, and then often *talked to their partners* (or themselves) in an amazed reaction as they recognized how fast all those numbers were adding up. After this experience and special sensory awareness, it didn't take long to change behavior and thinking regarding their spending.

After using this manual method for a few months, recording the expenses, as well as planning the unique monthly variations, you will gain some valuable insights. *At this point, it does make sense to transition to the convenience of budgeting electronically.* Using the concepts, categories, and formats in this workbook will supplement whatever electronic system or program you use and will help you develop a more effective spending plan.

One reader summed it up the best: *"I have tried many other books. This is the only book I have found that enabled me to keep track so completely. It also helped me understand the basic concepts first before I moved on to the computer level. Thank you for offering such a practical system."*

What about the Dual Household?

These past few years, I have noticed more couples who were getting stuck with their "method of choice" when it came to going electronic or staying manual. Each was stubbornly holding on to their method of choice and just as stubbornly resisting the method used by their partner. What to do? The best solution for my clients has been to use *BOTH*!

Once you are no longer putting energy into defending why your method is better, you each can focus on getting the budget done. It may seem a bit redundant, but in the end, both partners are involved in their own way and they are taking more time to communicate and collaborate so their numbers and records are accurate. The ultimate goals of getting a handle on spending, getting out of debt, and saving more money are eventually accomplished—and with less friction.

In many cases, one of the transition options was to have one partner use the Excel version of *The Budget Kit* primary worksheets (*moneytracker.com/books-TheBudgetKitExcel.htm*) so they could still feel they were on the computer, and the other partner entered information into this workbook.

My motto is always "If it works, stay with it." You'll know when and if you are ready to change systems.

Take Charge of Your Life and Money

The methods and guidelines in this workbook will show you how to set your goals, watch your spending, plan your expenses, and save more money. You will then find that your bills are paid on time, more money is saved than you ever thought possible, your investments are off to a healthy start, your goals are being reached, and the stress in your life is reduced.

As you take charge of your money, you will notice this control carrying over to other aspects of your life. Your relationships with your family will become more relaxed, and more time will be available to pay attention to other things in life besides money.

Most importantly, you will begin to notice a new awareness of your priorities and values. *Paying attention to your finances in a more conscientious and deliberate way will help you see that your actions, beliefs, and results are in total alignment with your true life priorities and values.*

Best of luck as you begin your new money-management journey!

Living in a Cashless Society

Whether you fully embrace the Internet and the convenience of managing all your financial affairs electronically and online or you tend to resist going around cashless and prefer your tangible currency and checks, it's time to understand how the cashless society is affecting your life. Every financial transaction you make that does not involve an exchange of actual cash or a written check is essentially a cashless transaction. As the online process and wireless possibilities continue to evolve, these cashless transaction options are becoming ubiquitous.

Already, you may go through a day, a week, or a month without ever actually touching, exchanging, or seeing cash or checks. How does this method of operating with "invisible money" affect how you create and/or maintain a successful spending plan? And how does it affect your attitude about your spending?

For some, it has already become a nightmare as they try to manually balance various checking accounts and track multiple credit and debit cards and different online accounts to get a handle on how much is actually being spent. Without extreme discipline and a plan, it is nearly impossible to gather up and record, with any accuracy, all the loose pieces of financial information rolling away in unrecorded multiple ATM withdrawals, debit payments, automatic bank withdrawals, bank fees, and other online fees.

For others, who immediately appreciated the potential of the cashless option, heaven has just arrived on earth. At last they feel organized and efficient, have a convenient system that works, and know exactly where they stand financially at any given time.

How is this stream of plastic, electronic, and online options affecting your own financial situation?

Is Cashless Best for You?

For all the convenience of operating in a cashless society, the ultimate financial responsibility continues to rest on your shoulders. This means it is still up to you to research financial products and services, arrange the proper timing of bill payments, take precautions against identity theft in all areas of online financial information, and—last but not least—review and back up your accounts regularly.

As you operate in this convenient cashless style, are you still staying mindful of expenses and staying within some financial guidelines that outline specific limits? Or, as money becomes less tangible, do you notice yourself acting as though you have more money than you really do? Just because the cashless convenience is there and everyone seems to use it does not mean you have to operate in a cashless way.

If you know yourself well and realize you do not stay connected effectively to money and your financial situation when operating with only credit cards and online payment services, it may be better to revert back to cash, debit cards, and occasional checks to get back in touch with money and your spending plan.

Even though society is operating more and more on a cashless basis, more people at my workshops are sharing the idea of reverting back to the old-fashioned envelope system: using set amounts of cash in each envelope for specific categories like "meals out" or "entertainment." When the "meals out" cash envelope is empty, there is no more eating out for the remainder of that month. Now that's tangible!

How Does *The Budget Kit* Fit in with This Cashless Society?

Using any of the numerous personal finance software packages can certainly help you balance your checkbook, track your checking and savings accounts as well as your investments, pinpoint records you will need for taxes, and print out overflowing reports in every kind of chart, graph, and style you can imagine. Armed with all this information, you may feel like you are taking charge and feel totally in control, which you absolutely can be with such functional and powerful tools.

However, if you are noticing that your spending habits have not changed, your debt load has not come down, and you are still frustrated and not clear about your total financial picture, it may be time for a closer, hands-on review of the situation. Go through *The Budget Kit* sections, especially Part Two, and note any worksheets you previously used manually but are no longer using because of your new software or online program.

The bottom line when it comes to managing your money, whether manually or online, is still to have an effective, organized plan or system that you totally understand that gives you a comprehensive monthly and yearly financial picture. You want this picture to be realistic and based on accurate tracking and records (of all cash, checks, cashless transactions, and associated fees) so you know exactly where you stand financially at any time. You then can see immediately what adjustments, if any, you need to make to stay on course and within your budget guidelines.

The Budget Kit explains the basic concepts and steps in a simple, user-friendly format and gives you all the easy tools and worksheets you need for manually accomplishing all of these steps. Understanding these concepts is a critical first step before transferring over to *any* personal finance software or online system for peak efficiency and effectiveness.

As more and more new cashless methods of spending emerge and less physical contact is made with cash, it is easier to become further removed and out of touch with the reality of your financial situation. Having an understanding of the basic concepts and some kind of hands-on backup system in place, like *The Budget Kit,* keeps you in closer contact with your money and helps you better adjust to and track all the new technical and financial changes, charges, and records being introduced.

Ultimately, the real goal of blending the concepts of *The Budget Kit* with the conveniences of operating in a cashless society is to achieve some peace of mind. One way to gain that serenity is to pay your bills regularly and on time, which will also help you establish a strong credit history. A solid budget will ensure the availability of funds to make the payments. Online bill payment services, handled effectively, can dramatically improve your life in numerous ways. When you no longer have to face the draining monthly ritual of writing and mailing checks to pay bills, knowing they are all under control, you can start to shift your time and energy to focus on the more significant people and events in your life.

Online Budgeting, Banking, and Bill Payment

Online Budgeting

The Internet has certainly revolutionized how we live and manage our financial lives.

The online financial scene is changing so rapidly that I hesitate to mention website or product names anymore, knowing how quickly these services merge with others, morph into something new, or disappear altogether. As of this writing, there is certainly no shortage of excellent online budgeting programs and applications offered for free or minimal fees by banks, credit card companies, and independent website services.

Most of these products and services offer links for all of your accounts, even those accounts with other banks or lenders, so you can see all your information in one convenient place. Sorting options let you pinpoint specific transactions. Various budget programs can help you set budgets, monitor spending habits, and create reports. If you enjoy seeing colorful graphs and working with calculators, these tools are also available at most of the websites. Remember, reports are only as accurate as the information you provide or fail to provide. For your convenience, I've included a number of websites with calculator tools on page 107 under "Online Calculators."

The real question is, how are these creative financial changes and tools impacting your life and your own financial management system—or spotlighting your *lack* of a system?

Again, the key point is to be sure you have the foundation for understanding what to do with all this innovative, sophisticated information in terms of your own personal financial situation. This is once again where the concepts in *The Budget Kit* workbook come in.

Online Banking and Bill Payment

Of course not everyone has moved to online banking, but if you have, I'm sure you have noticed that upgrades and services, like offers for overdraft protection or credit report alerts, are introduced regularly. Banks are always looking for additional ways to generate revenue, so don't feel you need to bite on those offers. They may not be in your best interest.

If you use the concepts and tools in this workbook and have a solid financial spending plan in place, you won't need the expensive overdraft protection. Be proactive, take responsibility, and stay alert on a regular basis to your own online balances so you don't set yourself up for an overdraft situation in the first place. With all the latest mobile technology and the availability of up-to-the-minute information, paying attention to your balances is certainly more manageable than ever.

One of the advantages of the bill payment service is how efficiently it handles bills; another is that you know your balances immediately. Of course, the disadvantage is no longer having that "float time" of mail delivery. If you are combining paying bills online with writing paper checks, be sure to subtract the amount of any written checks that have not cleared the bank yet when reviewing your online balance.

In the case of combined online and written check payments, "balancing your checkbook" is still as important as it was in the paper checkbook days. What is different now, however, is the ease of balancing and controlling the checkbook with mobile banking and automatic email and text message alerts. All the alerts are there, ranging from "low balance" or "recent deposit" to "bill reminders" and "recent activity," to help you stay on top of your spending activity. You (or your partner, if dealing with a joint account) just need to take the time to set up those alerts and respond to them in a timely manner.

Keep in mind that if you have a joint account, your most effective strategy is basic communication. Perhaps your partner pays a number of the bills at one time, knowing the money is there, and fails to mention this to you. Before using your joint account to make a number of *spontaneous, unplanned debits,* the best way to prevent any overdrafts (or emotional triggers) is not only to check your online balance but to check in with your partner regarding any pending checks.

Will My Money Be Safe If I Bank Online?

Worrying about having all of your personal financial information exposed on the Internet is not unfounded. Established banks and companies have been well aware of the potential danger. Consequently, due to the enormous need for security when dealing with this level of personal financial information, these businesses use the highest level of security currently available in the industry. Read through the security information thoroughly on your bank's website and any other websites where you store financial information to learn how they handle security.

These financial institutions want to make sure they are providing a secure site for you while you are visiting and using their websites. You will often see text on Internet sites that states your account information and transactions are being protected by encryption using SSL (Secure Sockets Layer) technology. Basically, when your account information is passing back and forth between two different secure websites, or your computer and a secure website, encryption is a technology that totally scrambles every bit of information, so it is impossible to decipher during the transmission time. It's a little like our Navajo "code talkers" during WWII who spoke in Navajo as they passed the highest security information back and forth and who could not be understood by *any* other country.

Encryption prevents any party from intercepting the information and prevents eavesdropping, tampering, or forged messages while the information is not yet secured inside a protected website.

Always watch for the little icons (usually yellow) that look like padlocks, usually located on the status bar on the website. If you look to the right of the address bar in Microsoft Explorer, you will see the padlock icon. When you click on this icon, information will show up to explain the level of security being used. Another way to look for security is to watch for a website URL that begins with *https*. The *s* stands for *secure.*

Financial websites provide more security and help protect your privacy by logging you out of the online banking service after so many minutes of inactivity. This is a very safe precaution. It also can be a frustrating one if you are in the middle of setting up a transaction and suddenly need to dig through some files to find a specific detail, only to return and notice you have been logged out and all the previous work you put in was erased. A good habit to establish when finished on a website is to *log off as soon as you have completed working on your accounts and close your browser.*

Privacy Issues

You may be asking, What about identity theft? Again, your fears are valid. Identity theft happens when someone gains access to and uses your personal information, such as your name, drivers license, Social Security number, birth date, credit card number, or other identifying information, without your permission to make purchases or to commit fraud or other crimes. This is another reason you want to be very careful when setting up user names and passwords. Be especially careful about keeping this information private and in a safe place.

Protecting your financial records is enormously important for preserving your privacy. *Monitor your online records and reports regularly to be sure you recognize all the transactions.* At the same time, remember that your regular mail is still intensely sought after by mail thieves, so check your bank and credit card statements often to watch for any mail tampering. Better yet, change to paperless so you can preserve a tree while protecting your identity.

You also can take an active part in preventing fraud by periodically reviewing your credit report. See the **Credit Bureaus and Identity Theft Hotline** section on page 22. These credit bureaus will provide you with a credit report for a small fee.

If you are extremely concerned about protecting your identity and credit, you may want to sign up for an email notification service that will alert you whenever your credit profiles change. Services are available through the credit reporting agencies, your bank, Identity Theft Shield (through Pre-Paid Legal Services Inc.), and numerous other credit-monitoring companies.

However, I would be very cautious when signing up for any of these services. Be sure you know (and ask) exactly what services you are and *are not* receiving. Does the service search public records, online directories, and Internet chat rooms for your personal information such as your Social Security number, credit and debit cards, or online bank accounts and then apprise you of any compromised personal information? Is there a limit to how many accounts it will monitor? Are phone consult services available without charge?

Some services may alert you of changes but not do much to assist you with an actual identity theft situation. Don't overlook the recovery assistance service question. By now you've heard how extremely expensive, time-consuming, and frustrating identity theft can be. If the service you select prevents a theft attempt or assists you through the entire recovery process, then that monthly or annual fee will be well worth it.

The best insurance is still doing your part to protect yourself from fraud or identity theft in the first place. See **Top 12 List of How to Protect Yourself from Fraud and Identity Theft** and **Online Resources—Identity Theft and Fraud Hotlines**, which follow, for more suggestions.

Top 12 List of How to Protect Yourself from Fraud and Identity Theft

1. Avoid ever giving out your entire Social Security number (SSN), the last four digits of your SSN, your birth date, your mother's maiden name, any financial account numbers, credit card three-digit verification number, or your password by phone, in the mail, or online *if you did not initiate the contact, do not know the caller, or did not type in the website address.*

2. Stay suspicious with calls sounding professional and helpful from financial-related companies or "Security and Fraud Departments." If they verify much of your personal information and only need you to provide information on one or two items, do not give out this information. *Call this company back on a number you already have or look them up* (statements, phone book, Internet) and then verify if this call was valid. If you DID give out critical information, file a police report right away.

3. Stay alert for "phishing" (an email fraud scam where the message looks like it came from a legitimate and trustworthy bank, business, or online organization asking for your personal and financial information for various purposes). Never click on hyperlinks or cut and paste these links from any suspicious or unknown emails. *Go directly to the website instead and log into your account.*

4. Shield your card information while waiting in line or during a transaction and shield your hand at an ATM machine. *Someone can be photographing your card or videotaping your password hand motions from a distance.*

5. Pay attention to late or missing bills and *any credit cards you never applied for.* Follow up immediately.

6. Collect your mail right away. *Do not let mail received or outgoing mail sit in an unsecured mailbox.*

7. *Do not carry your Social Security card, passport, or multiple credit cards* on you when not needed.

8. If you are still using checks and order new ones, pick them up at the bank. *Do NOT have them mailed to an unsecured mailbox at your home.*

9. Shred all credit card offers and all other financial papers *showing any of your personal and account number information.*

10. *Install a reputable firewall* on your computer and *keep it upgraded.* Before you dispose of your computer, delete all stored personal information. Programs that can destroy your data and delete the files on your hard drive are called "drive wipe" or "data erase" programs. Since technology changes so rapidly, keep in mind that this terminology may change, and even this suggestion may become out-of-date. Look for a reputable software review and download site such as *www.download.com*, which will give you a list of programs with editor and user ratings and brief descriptions, rather than using a more general search engine like Google. Some possible websites to explore are *www.tucows.com* and *www.snapfiles.com*.

11. If you inadvertently give out critical personal information or become a victim of identity theft, contact one of the three consumer credit-reporting agencies listed (see **Credit Bureaus and Identity Theft Hotline** box) and *place an initial fraud alert* on your credit reports right away. *Close the tampered or fraudulent accounts, file a complaint with the FTC, and file a report with the police.* You can also request a security freeze on your credit file at any time.

12. *Continue to monitor your credit reports and statements.* Watch for any new fraudulent accounts. Some thieves will wait months until you feel safe again before using your information.

If you feel you may be a victim of identity theft, contact the Federal Trade Commission's Identity Theft Hotline toll-free at 877-ID-THEFT (877-438-4338), or visit the U.S. government's central website for information about identity theft at *www.ftc.gov/bcp/edu/microsites/idtheft*.

Identity Theft—Online Resources and Fraud Hotlines

- Federal Trade Commission (FTC)
  Identity theft: *www.ftc.gov/bcp/edu/microsites/idtheft*; 877-438-4338
  Consumer complaints: *www.ftccomplaintassistant.gov*
  Money management and scam alerts: *www.ftc.gov/moneymatters*

- U.S. Department of Justice
  Identity theft: *www.justice.gov/criminal/fraud/websites/idtheft.html*; (202) 514-7023
  Office of Justice programs: *http://ojp.usdoj.gov/programs/identitytheft.htm*

- National Association of Attorneys General
  Attorneys General for each state: *http://naag.org/current-attorneys-general.php*

- Social Security Administration
  Fraud hotline: *www.socialsecurity.gov/oig/hotline/index.htm*; 800-269-0271

- U.S. Postal Inspection Service
  Mail fraud, including identity theft: *https://postalinspectors.uspis.gov*; 888-877-7644

- Internal Revenue Service
  "Identity Theft and Your Tax Records": *www.irs.gov/privacy/article/0,,id=186436,00.html*; 800-829-0433

- National Crime Prevention Council
  www.ncpc.org; (202) 466-6272
  "Preventing Identity Theft: A Guide for Consumers": *www.ncpc.org/resources/files/pdf/fraud/idtheftrev.pdf*

- Identity Theft Resource Center
  www.idtheftcenter.org
  Victim assistance hotline: 888-400-5530
  Questions: (858) 693-7935

- 101 Identity Theft—Prevention and Victim Information
  www.101-identitytheft.com

Opt-Out Option

One last note on privacy. Remember to watch for opt-out choices in the literature or online when you are setting up your service with any company, including your financial institution, phone, utility, and credit card companies. Opt-out means you are opting out of receiving any information or direct marketing materials unrelated to your account from that company itself. They will also assure you that your information is not being shared with any outside companies. Be sure to fill out the necessary paperwork or make the phone call to initiate this choice. This is your responsibility.

Opt-Out Resources

Use these resources for getting your name off of email lists and lists of direct marketing, telemarketing, credit bureaus, lenders, and many more.

- Consumer Credit Reporting Industry
  www.optoutprescreen.com; 888-5-OPT-OUT (888-567-8688)

- Direct Marketing Association
  Stop preapproved credit card mail offers:

  Direct Marketing Association
  Mail Preference Service
  PO Box 643
  Carmel, NY 10512
  www.dmachoice.org

  This site also offers an email preference service (eMPS) to remove your email from national lists.

- Federal Trade Commission (FTC)
  "Sharing Your Personal Information: It's Your Choice": *www.ftc.gov/privacy/protect.shtm*

- FTC National Do Not Call Registry
  Information: *www.ftc.gov/bcp/edu/microsites/donotcall/index.html*
  Registration: *www.donotcall.gov*; 888-382-1222

  Your registration will not expire. Telephone numbers placed on the National Do Not Call Registry will remain on it permanently due to the Do-Not-Call Improvement Act of 2007, which became law in February 2008. This registry is enforced by the FTC, the Federal Communications Commission (FCC), and state law enforcement officials.

- Privacy Rights Clearing House
  Consumer form letters and opt-out information: *www.privacyrights.org/letters/letters.htm*

Credit Reports and FICO Scores

Your credit score now has a more significant impact on your financial life than ever before. A low score could be costing you hundreds of dollars with higher interest rates on your mortgage, car payment, and credit cards. It can also impact rates for your health and car insurance as well as interfere with your search for employment and a place to rent.

Take advantage of the free annual credit reports available from all three credit-reporting agencies by staggering these requests throughout the year. There are additional ways to receive a free credit report. Your rights through the federal Fair Credit Reporting Act (FCRA) entitle you to a free report if a company has denied your application for credit, insurance, or employment because of information in a report (you must request the report within 60 days of receiving the notice); if your report is inaccurate because of fraud, including identity theft; if you are on welfare; or if you are unemployed but expect to apply for employment within 60 days. Visit *www.ftc.gov/credit* for a wealth of additional information.

Be very wary of any media ads for free credit reports, and stay alert to the preponderance of scams online, through the mail, and on TV. Most of these companies will ask for your credit card number ahead of time, require a monthly subscription, and give you only basic data, requiring extra fees for scores. Also, there is no guarantee the score you receive is the official FICO score.

One way you can count on getting your real FICO score is by applying for a mortgage or mortgage prequalification. On that note, be aware that the free annual credit reports apply to you and your spouse *individually*. Your scores are not "married," meaning both of your scores are not totaled and then divided by two. This can have a major impact if you are applying for a mortgage loan together. The low score of just one spouse could sabotage the loan for both.

To order your free credit report and get more information, visit *www. annualcreditreport.com;* call 877-322-8228; or write to Annual Credit Report Request Service, PO Box 105281, Atlanta, GA 30348-5281. Another resource is *www.myfico.com.*

Note: As this book goes to press, the three credit reporting agencies are going through some changes, so be on the lookout for new information at these websites.

Credit Bureaus and Identity Theft Hotline

The current three credit reporting agencies as of this printing are:

1. Experian: 888-397-3742,
   www.experian.com

2. Equifax: 800-685-1111,
   www.equifax.com

3. TransUnion: 800-916-8800,
   www.transunion.com

Once you do receive a credit report, it's important to realize these reports often contain a high percentage of wrong information, whether due to data entry errors or any number of other reasons, including illegal use of your credit or identity. Review your reports thoroughly and watch for suspicious activity. Report corrections immediately.

It also doesn't hurt to review your credit report more than once a year, especially if you actively use a number of different credit cards, have recently taken out a loan, or have moved. Since the information on these credit reports is seldom static in our fast-changing financial world, checking your credit report only once a year may no longer be sound financial management. Paying the nominal agency fee a few times a year could ultimately save you a great deal more, not only in terms of your money but also your time and emotional energy.

There are numerous sources for more thorough information regarding your credit report and FICO scores available online, in the library, and through other books. Stay current with this information. The guidelines on how your credit score is affected have been changing dramatically over the last few years. With the ongoing rapid changes in the credit world, you can no longer depend on the accuracy of information you may have learned years ago.

Remember that one of the best and basic ways to gradually improve your score and keep your score high is to make all your payments *on time* and *in full*.

On the other hand, if you pride yourself on not using credit (an admirable policy), this lack of credit history and activity can actually work against you when you want to apply for a home or vehicle loan. One quick way to establish some credit history is to deposit a small amount of money into your bank or credit union and then arrange to take out a loan for the same amount. Set up an automatic payment program with low monthly payments for this loan, using the money you just deposited. The goal is to establish some credit history using an *installment loan,* which will be recorded accordingly with the credit bureaus. You want an installment loan rather than a debt that is *due in full.* This will benefit the Payment History part of your FICO scores. See the FICO Score Calculations section that follows.

FICO Score Calculations

Know the basics of what impacts your score the most.

35%—Payment History

Late payments, including payments below the minimum requirement, have a huge hit on your score. The more recent the late payment, the lower the score on your report. The total number of delinquent accounts also matters.

30%—Outstanding Debt

This evaluates how close you are to the credit limit on any account. Keep smaller balances spread out over more cards, rather than maxing out one card by consolidating all debt on that card.

15%—Credit History

Do not close old cards if you've had them for many years and they show a long history for you, even if you have not had any activity on that card for awhile—especially if you do not have many other cards showing any credit history. Closing cards used to be the advice in the past, but this is no longer the case. The object is to show a long established history of credit and timely payments. If you close any accounts, close your newest accounts.

10%—Type of Credit

This evaluates the mix of credit, including installment loans, mortgages, leases, credit cards, etc. Finance company credit is one of the most negative. A mixture of credit accounts generates a better score than only having numerous credit cards.

10%—Inquiries

Every inquiry by credit promotions, employers, credit card applications, bank reviews, etc. shows up on your credit report. Be aware that not all inquiries are treated the same. The time lapse since recent inquiries or newly opened accounts also makes a difference.

Online Information Record

Keeping track of all the different information you need to log on to secure Internet sites can be daunting. If you haven't already come up with some system for keeping all those personal user names and passwords in one place, use this **Online Information Record** to gather your information together.

A word of caution: if you are using online banking and other online financial services and have most of your financial records stored online, be extremely careful to keep your password and PIN information private. Your PIN confirms your identity and unlocks the access to your accounts.

Decide who will have access to this information. Do not give this information to anyone or leave it where someone can easily see it or find it. At the same time, be sure the appropriate members of your family have access or know where and how to get access to this information. Not only is this important during an emergency, but it preserves the balance of knowledge and power in the family.

Protect your PIN and password as carefully as you would your ATM PIN. As an extra precaution, periodically change your password and PIN number.

After you fill out this form, it is a good idea to tear out these pages and keep them in a very secure place.

ONLINE INFORMATION RECORD

WEBSITE NAME AND WEB ADDRESS	USER NAME/ID	PASSWORD	PIN/OTHER #

ACCOUNT #	PASSWORD HINT—Q/A	CUSTOMER/TECH SUPPORT #	NOTES

Part One

One longtime reader wrote to say: "When I started keeping records it was like an awakening. In seven years, I saved $100,000 thanks to your book. By the end of this year, which will be just over nine years, that number should be close to a quarter of a million." It's amazing how the numbers start to accelerate after a certain point.

This reader was exceptionally disciplined and motivated. Whenever he did not spend money (e.g., walk versus taxi, video versus movie, library versus bookstore), he would actually put that savings aside and record it in his book. On last conversation, he still continues to feel no deprivation. He now *knows* he can buy anything he wants and is very satisfied with how he chooses to spend his money.

As you fill in the following pages in Part One, you will see more clearly what you already have and what you still would like to have.

Writing down what you want in black and white is always a powerful way of becoming more focused and motivated in your daily living. Part Two will give you the tools for accomplishing your goals.

Another reader wrote to say:

"I thought you might like an update. I think you will remember me—the one who lived in a black hole as far as money was concerned. ("Do people really DO this?" I asked you.)

"Well, I am happy to report that light permeates that hole now! And I am even having fun budgeting! I really like it! I now know where all our money goes. I watch it and record what is happening where and when. I look ahead and plan and save.

"SAVE—what a word. It is great to plan ahead and save a portion of our income for a future expense. AND—it was an eye-opener to see the waste. Money that was wasted is now being conserved and used wisely. We even had a reserve to buy Christmas presents for a family of five who needed clothes, books, and toys. It felt wonderful to do that anonymously and get our children involved in helping out someone less fortunate.

Net Worth Statement

Identified Goals Worksheet

Goals Savings Record

Needs/Wants List

"We saved and then spent $24,000 on energy efficiency on the house from our salaries. (We get 25 percent back from the feds when we are finished.) We plugged up the holes where money was leaking from us.

"There are so many ways to save money. We joined Sam's Club to save money by buying in bulk discount. (We already have a neighborhood food co-op.) We spent $2,000 LESS on Christmas this year by being aware of what was going on, having a budget, and then sticking to it. We renewed our library cards and frequent the library.

"I feel as if blinders have been lifted off me! I didn't even know what I earned!"

—Julie H., NY

Net Worth Statement

An important step in gaining financial control is to take an accounting of what your total financial worth is. Every year, when you tabulate your net worth, it will enable you to review your progress and compare it with your financial goals. A net worth statement is a snapshot of your current financial situation; therefore, it changes over time. In addition, a net worth statement is a valuable aid in planning your estate and establishing a record for loan and insurance purposes.

Keep in mind that the value of your assets can change dramatically, especially during turbulent economic times such as those we recently experienced. This is another reason you want to pay close attention to your personal finances.

On the following **Net Worth Statement** worksheet, total up all your assets (what you OWN). Next, total up all your liabilities (what you OWE). Subtract the amount of the liabilities total from the assets total to calculate your total net worth. Ideally, you will have a positive figure.

Your goal is to have a positive net worth that increases each year or recovers as quickly as possible from a drop during a challenging economy.

NET WORTH STATEMENT

ASSETS—WHAT YOU OWN

	Amount
Cash: On Hand	_____
Checking Accounts	_____
Savings Accounts	_____
Money Markets	_____
Other	_____
Real Estate/Property (current market value):	
Principal Residence	_____
Second Residence	_____
Land	_____
Income Property	_____
Other (business, partnerships, etc.)	_____
Investments (market value):	
Cash Value Life Insurance	_____
Certificates of Deposit	_____
U.S. Treasury Bills/Savings Bonds	_____
Stocks	_____
Bonds	_____
Mutual Funds	_____
College Fund (529 Plans, etc.)	_____
Limited Partnerships	_____
Annuities	_____
IRA–Regular/Roth	_____
Keogh/SEP Plans	_____
401(k), 403(b), or 457 Plans	_____
Pension Plan/Retirement Plans	_____
Other (stock options, bonuses, etc.)	_____
Personal Loans Receivable	_____
Personal Property (current market value):	
Cars, Trucks, Vehicles	_____
Recreational Vehicle/Watercraft	_____
Electronic Equipment	_____
Home Furnishings	_____
Home Entertainment	_____
Equipment/Tools	_____
Appliances and Furniture	_____
Collectibles/Antiques	_____
Jewelry and Furs	_____
Other:	_____
Total Assets	$ _____

LIABILITIES—WHAT YOU OWE

	Amount
Current Debts:	
Household	_____
Medical	_____
Credit Card 1	_____
Credit Card 2	_____
Credit Card 3	_____
Department Store Cards	_____
Back Taxes (Federal, State, Property)	_____
Legal	_____
Child Support	_____
Alimony	_____
Other:	_____
Other:	_____
Mortgages:	
Principal Residence	_____
Second Residence	_____
Land	_____
Income Property	_____
Other:	_____
Other:	_____
Loans:	
Home Equity (HELOC)	_____
Bank/Finance Company	_____
Automobiles, Vehicles	_____
Recreational Vehicle/Watercraft	_____
Education/Student	_____
Life Insurance	_____
Personal (from family or friends)	_____
Retirement Accounts	_____
Thrift Savings Plan	_____
Other:	_____
	_____
	_____
	_____
Total Liabilities	$ _____

Total Assets		Total Liabilities		Net Worth
$ _____	–	$ _____	=	$ _____

Setting Financial Goals

Jan was never successful at saving even though she made a great income as a loan officer. Once she started tracking her spending and learned how to work out a budget, it made a "million percent" difference in her life. She created a savings account to buy a house, which she never could do before. She practiced the "pay yourself first" technique, considered her savings as a bill, and successfully saved $15,000 in one year and bought her house. Now she's even more motivated about saving and is planning to invest in additional real estate.

Setting financial goals is one of the most important steps for gaining financial control. When you have a goal, you have the motivation needed to follow a money-management plan.

The worksheets on the following pages will help you identify and record your financial goals and develop a plan for reaching them.

To begin, ask yourself what is important to you. What will make you happy and/or be a significant accomplishment? Define your goals in specific attainable terms (such as buying a red two-door BMW instead of just buying a new car), and write them down. You then have taken the first step toward reaching your goals.

You can find more goal-setting information with a search on Amazon or Google.

Immediate/Short-Range Goals

These goals are any that you have identified for the next month and/or year. Your goals depend on your interests and your lifestyle. Perhaps you want to save your Christmas money in advance this year, buy the latest tablet/eReader, or pay off a major debt.

Do not forget your emergency fund. If you do not have at least three to six (or even eight) months' take-home pay set aside as a protection against unforeseen problems or disasters, this should be your *number-one goal*. Once you have the security of knowing you are covered for possible emergencies, you can comfortably focus on your other goals.

"I opened a savings account several months ago, and I'm having a small amount deducted monthly from my checking account. I already can see the effect you're talking about, as I find myself NOT touching the savings account, since it is my emergency account, and just paying with the cash I have or figuring out a less expensive way to get what I need and want."

—Diane, NM

When you reach the goals you have identified in this section, you will have more confidence and discipline for the more aggressive goals in the Middle- and Long-Range Goals section.

Middle- and Long-Range Goals

Middle-range goals are those you hope to reach two to five years from now. Maybe you are dreaming of a new home, thinking of starting a family, or planning a trip abroad.

Long-range goals include plans beyond five years, including college tuition and retirement. By thinking about longer-range periods, you will make wiser use of your money. With time on your side, small amounts of money saved regularly for 10 to 40 years will grow tremendously. And if you pay closer attention to where you invest your money, it could grow even more.

Family Affair

If you have a family, bring everyone together to discuss their interests and goals. Children benefit from taking part in this activity not only to give their input, but to learn from the process for their own adult years.

There seldom is enough money to reach everyone's goals. When Dad wants the latest HDTV, Mom wants a new refrigerator, and your teen wants the latest video game, compromise is necessary. Each member of the family learns to give and take and decide what is agreeable as a compromise. Rather than drop a major goal altogether, try extending the deadline date.

One family decided to cut back and save for a car. In two and a half years' time, this family of four with two young children saved $18,000. They did not feel deprived when they chose to cut back on clothing and eating out and did a lot more buying at garage sales and auctions. Each month they also invested $300 without exception in a mutual fund as a dollar cost average approach. The best part was feeling confident in their ability to actually pull it off.

Filling in Your Identified Goals Worksheet

Once you have defined your goals and have written them down under "Goals" on the **Identified Goals Worksheet** on page 35, fill in the remainder of the worksheet. Number the "Priority" of each goal listed. Which goal do you want first, second, and so on? Which can wait a few months or another year?

What is your "Target Date"? Six months, one year, six years? Every goal should have a beginning and an ending date. Once you have committed yourself to a time frame in your mind and on paper, you have taken one more positive step toward reaching your goal.

"Cost Estimate" helps develop your estimating ability and forces you to do some research. By calling, reading, or shopping online to determine the estimated cost of new energy-efficient windows or solar panels, for example, your goal becomes more than just a dream.

If you have money in savings, how much of that "Amount Already Saved" do you want to use toward your goal? Write it down. Commit yourself to an amount.

"How to Achieve" is crucial. What are you willing to do to make your goal a reality? Will it involve working overtime or finding a second job? Will it mean trade-offs—cutting back or eliminating expenses such as movies, meals out, or smoking—so you can reach your goal?

How much will you have to save each week, month, or year to reach your goals? If you have a difficult time setting aside money for your goals, arrange with your bank for direct deposit from your paycheck.

The **Goals Savings Record** on page 36 is a great place for keeping track of your savings for your goals. Take your "Cost Estimate" figure from the **Identified Goals Worksheet** and write it in the space next to "Total Cost." If you want this goal in one year, divide that figure by 12 to see how much money you need to save every month. Each month, record your savings and balance. You will be excited to actually see yourself coming closer to your goal.

Pay Attention to Your Money

If you have a strong desire to reach your goal and you *really* want your money to work for you, it's very important to pay attention to what you do with your money.

Earlier, I mentioned having time on your side and paying closer attention to your money. For long-range goals (college, early retirement) where large amounts are necessary, these two factors are critical.

Let's say that you decide to save $100 at the beginning of every month for ten years to reach your goal. You could stash that money under your favorite mattress and have $12,000 at the end of ten years. Obviously, that method may not be the wisest or safest.

If you had chosen to take that monthly $100 to your bank and let it sit safely in a savings account and draw 3 to 5 percent compounded daily interest, after ten years you would have made nearly $2,000 to $3,500 "free" dollars for doing nothing more than driving to your local bank or transferring online. In the meantime, you would have saved $15,536.81 for your goal.

On the other hand, if you were to take time to find an account that pays 10 percent compounded daily interest for that same $100 every month for ten years, your reward for your research time would be an extra $4,995.61 over the 5 percent interest from the bank, or an extra $8,532.42 over the mattress investment, giving you $20,532.42 for your goal!

Saving $100 a Month for Ten Years

	Under the Mattress	*3–5% Interest*	*10% Interest*
Total Saved	$12,000	$15,536.81	$20,532.42

These figures do not include inflation or rare economic events; however, the more years you have to invest and the higher interest rate or return amount you get, the more money you will ultimately make. Read financial books, newspapers, and magazines, surf the Web, or talk to your financial planner, broker, accountant, or local banker to examine your options. *When you learn how to effectively invest your hard-earned money, you can be more confident that you will reach your goals.*

IDENTIFIED GOALS WORKSHEET

IMMEDIATE/SHORT-RANGE GOALS

Priority	Goal	Target Date	Cost Estimate	Amount Already Saved	How to Achieve (amount per month, second job, etc.)

MIDDLE- AND LONG-RANGE GOALS

Priority	Goal	Target Date	Cost Estimate	Amount Already Saved	How to Achieve (amount per month, second job, etc.)

GOALS SAVINGS RECORD

Goal: Roth IRA

Total Cost: 3,500

	JAN.	FEB.	MAR.	APR.	MAY	JUNE	JULY	AUG.	SEPT.	OCT.	NOV.	DEC.	
Deposit	292	292	250	275	350	292	270	320	292	292	290	285	Monthly Avg. Deposit: 292
Balance	292	584	834	1,109	1,459	1,751	2,021	2,341	2,633	2,925	3,215	3,500	**Total:** 3,500

Goal:

Total Cost:

	JAN.	FEB.	MAR.	APR.	MAY	JUNE	JULY	AUG.	SEPT.	OCT.	NOV.	DEC.	
Deposit													Monthly Avg. Deposit:
Balance													**Total:**

Goal:

Total Cost:

	JAN.	FEB.	MAR.	APR.	MAY	JUNE	JULY	AUG.	SEPT.	OCT.	NOV.	DEC.	
Deposit													Monthly Avg. Deposit:
Balance													**Total:**

Goal:

Total Cost:

	JAN.	FEB.	MAR.	APR.	MAY	JUNE	JULY	AUG.	SEPT.	OCT.	NOV.	DEC.	
Deposit													Monthly Avg. Deposit:
Balance													**Total:**

Goal:

Total Cost:

	JAN.	FEB.	MAR.	APR.	MAY	JUNE	JULY	AUG.	SEPT.	OCT.	NOV.	DEC.	
Deposit													Monthly Avg. Deposit:
Balance													**Total:**

Goal:

Total Cost:

	JAN.	FEB.	MAR.	APR.	MAY	JUNE	JULY	AUG.	SEPT.	OCT.	NOV.	DEC.	
Deposit													Monthly Avg. Deposit:
Balance													**Total:**

Goal:

Total Cost:

	JAN.	FEB.	MAR.	APR.	MAY	JUNE	JULY	AUG.	SEPT.	OCT.	NOV.	DEC.	
Deposit													Monthly Avg. Deposit:
Balance													**Total:**

Goal:

Total Cost:

	JAN.	FEB.	MAR.	APR.	MAY	JUNE	JULY	AUG.	SEPT.	OCT.	NOV.	DEC.	
Deposit													Monthly Avg. Deposit:
Balance													**Total:**

Goal:

Total Cost:

	JAN.	FEB.	MAR.	APR.	MAY	JUNE	JULY	AUG.	SEPT.	OCT.	NOV.	DEC.	
Deposit													Monthly Avg. Deposit:
Balance													**Total:**

The formula for determining the monthly amount to save for each of your goals is:
Total cost of your goal ÷ Number of months left to date needed = Amount per month you need to save.

Needs/Wants List

"I absolutely LOVE your book. I cannot tell you how many times I have referenced it. I have things highlighted, I jot notes in the margins, and could not have turned my life around without it. I've focused on needs vs. wants... I have stuck with my 'needs only' shopping and feel so much better! I have slowly but surely begun to save, once again. It's been years since I've had money to put away into savings."

—Kerri H., IA

Taking Further Control of Finances

This **Needs/Wants List** on page 40 is like a "wish list" that helps you take financial control one step further. This section is designed to be a guideline for those times when you have extra money but want to be sure that you wisely use your money on priority items versus impulse items.

Needs and Wants versus Goals

Needs, wants, and goals as used in this workbook are all the things that you would like to have but generally take a back seat to making sure all your required needs are handled first. With your improved budgeting skills and money awareness, however, it's encouraging to know you will have the capability to eventually acquire these items.

The difference between needs and wants and goals is primarily in the cost and the significance of the desired items. Goals are more significant plans involving time and the gradual accumulation of funds for major purchases, such as a home theater system, car, or home. Elimination of a major debt is also a goal.

Needs and wants, on the other hand, are the smaller-ticket items. These are the purchases made when extra money (known as discretionary money) is left over after paying the bills and putting aside money for your savings and your goals.

How to Use This List

Throughout the year, you probably see or think about many things you need or would like to have but don't have the extra cash at the time to buy. Jot down all your ideas on this **Needs/Wants List**.

Items on your list can range from things seen on websites, in mail-order catalogs, TV advertisements, or stores to activities such as a Cirque du Soleil performance or a ski weekend. Having these ideas written down will also make it easier for you to remember to watch for sales and list gift ideas as they come up.

At the same time, make a check mark either under the "Need" (necessities for your everyday well-being, such as food, housing, or medicine) or "Want" (which are nice to have, such as the latest iPod, jewelry, or theater tickets, but which you can do without if you have to) column. This way, you can make sure you take care of needs first when extra money is available. Record the source and cost of your items. When you are ready to purchase the listed item, the necessary information will be handy.

By using this **Needs/Wants List**, you start establishing priorities and identifying what you really do want when you have extra money. When you have an extra $50 (which you determine after completing your **Monthly Budget Worksheet** in Part Two) and a sale suddenly catches your eye, you won't be so apt to impulsively buy something. It will be easier to remember when extra money is available that there was something else you really wanted or needed more.

A Family Affair

The ability to prioritize is a valuable skill for all age levels. If your children ask for something when money is tight, write down their wishes on the list or have the children write them down. Your action assures your children that you are *acknowledging* their needs and wants rather than saying that they just can't have something or that you "can't afford it." Remember that you are constantly being a role model with all of your words and actions. These are all subtle ways of setting the tone and message for how your child may view and handle finances as an adult. In this way, children also learn to establish priorities, make choices, and develop patience along with delayed gratification—all skills valuable for adulthood.

When money does become available, either from your budget or from gifts or other money sources, your children gain the skills of learning to choose which item on the list to buy based on cost and priority instead of reacting impulsively to the first temptation that catches their eye in the mall, on TV, or on the Internet.

One final note about children and money: For years, parents have been lamenting the lack of money education in the schools. Fortunately, we now have access to a wealth of valuable information from expert personal finance authors, university extension services, and numerous other agencies and organizations. It is available in books, in pamphlets, and on websites. There is also no shortage of articles on how parents can teach children of all ages how to save, spend, and share money. An Internet search will turn up numerous websites designed for kids, offering hands-on experience with handling and tracking their allowance and gift money and more. A great starting point would be a search on Janet Bodnar, editor of *Kiplinger's Personal Finance* magazine and author of several books about kids and money.

> *"The most profound result of using your tracking system is discovering how many OLD IDEAS we had about our spending/income. We are retired, with a good fixed income. After a lifetime of buying what we wanted/needed within reason, but often impulsively, we have a lot of tired old ideas and a sense of long-standing entitlement about how we live and what we buy. We had a mentality of instant gratification along with a mistaken and vague impression that we knew approximately what we had and how we could spend. After just two and a half months of accurate accounting, we see clearly (and are surprised) to discover where we spend impulsively and in what categories we mistake our wants for our needs. Thanks so much for your work! I would recommend your system to anyone."*
>
> —Margaret M., CA

NEEDS/WANTS LIST

PARENTS

Date	Item	Need	Want	Source (store, catalog, Internet, other)	Cost

CHILDREN

Date	Item	Need	Want	Source (store, catalog, Internet, other)	Cost

Part Two

"As a student, I used to carry my Budget Kit *workbook with me every day in my pack. For anyone not used to figures, this workbook is an easy way to start. When I wrote things down every day it made me think, 'Do I really need this?' 'Where could I save?' 'Is there something I'd rather spend my money on?' Writing everything down and seeing the total picture clearly gave me those answers and a real incentive to change."*

Now that you are ready to develop a spending plan (a budget), let me walk you through the process just as if I were sitting with you at your dining room table, as I do with my clients.

Please note: *The concepts, information, and worksheets presented here in Part Two are designed to apply to the majority of financial situations. This includes those unique changing economic events such as being laid off, living temporarily on unemployment, dealing with a reduced salary, going through a bankruptcy, adjusting to becoming a solo-preneur, as well as operating on a very fixed and limited income. In fact, the concepts presented here are almost more critical during those times and events than when you feel secure with a steady, stable income.*

The three sections on the right, **Yearly Budget Worksheet (Non-Monthly Anticipated Expenses)**, **Monthly Budget Worksheet**, and **Monthly Expense Record**, form the keystone for the whole budgeting process for all households. These three fundamental worksheets were developed for the original workbook in 1980. The other forms are supplemental worksheets added over the years for households with varying financial needs and situations. Over the years as I have worked with clients and talked with readers using this workbook, I have found that using these three core worksheets in this order has provided the most significant results.

For years, readers have had their favorite worksheets. Some used only one or two worksheets, where others used nearly all of them. The purpose of this revised workbook is still to give you the same flexibility to pick and choose the worksheets and sections that will work best for you. However, I want you to have the opportunity

Yearly Budget Worksheet (Non-Monthly Anticipated Expenses)

Suggestion List—Additional Non-Monthly Expenses

Gift Giving Worksheet

Christmas/Holiday Expense Worksheet

Monthly Budget Worksheet

Variable Income Worksheet

Windfall Planner

Multiple Sales Monthly Planner

Debt Payoff Record

Debt Repayment Worksheet

Credit Card Purchase Record

Monthly Expense Record

Summary-for-the-Year Record

to understand the sections early on so you don't overlook one that could be particularly valuable for you.

The **Yearly Budget Worksheet (Non-Monthly Anticipated Expenses)** is the *missing link* worksheet that I have found makes all the difference in the world for people, right from the beginning. By starting with this overall yearly picture of where your money periodically goes above and beyond the regular monthly bills and expenses, you see immediately and graphically why you are usually short each month, why you have so little to show for all the good money you make, or why your debt never seems to go down each year.

> *"I bought the previous edition of* The Budget Kit *and read the preface and prologue, and then it went into a pile with unopened mail and my action file that continued to grow. Recently I pulled the book off the shelf because I am at the point that I am ready to make a change. This time, I actually went to Part Two of the book and realized how well you had laid it out and how simply I could have started using this kit several years ago. Thank you for doing a great job in simplifying this subject."*
>
> —James R., FL

The **Monthly Budget Worksheet** is the next critical tool. As you begin each new month, use this worksheet to streamline the whole bill paying and budget planning process. This form helps you to anticipate all the bills as well as the majority of incidental expenses (hair coloring, child's field trip, dry cleaning, etc.) so you know and can project ahead of time (before the month even begins) how much money you will need for the entire month. You will immediately see if you are going to be short so you have time to start making some arrangements and changes. You will also know what you can and cannot afford in terms of impulsive splurge events.

At my workshops, I'll often start out by saying, "A budget will allow you to spend without guilt and save with more ease." In fact I had a client in California who used to say, "I love my budget; it allows me to keep my addiction." David hosts a podcast program of Brazilian music and knows exactly how much he can allocate to his CD purchases each week (usually $100/ week) or for the month. With that priority satisfied, he is happy to let go of other expenses and no longer spend impulsively.

The **Monthly Expense Record** is the final and most important tool that lets you know where all your money has *really gone* for the whole month. This is your reality check on what your spending habits (like the coffee and bagel, music downloads, apps, games, and books, etc.) are actually costing you.

These three core worksheets are available on Excel and look exactly like the worksheets in this section. They are available at *http://moneytracker.com/ books-TheBudgetKitExcel.htm* for a small additional fee.

What's the Difference between the Monthly Budget Worksheet and the Monthly Expense Record?

Of all the worksheets, these two seem to be the most confusing when people are just starting out—even after they've read or heard my explanation. I'm sure this is just human nature, especially if you're a bit overwhelmed looking at all these different worksheets for the first time. Be patient and take your time. Trust me, once you actually start using these two core worksheets the way they are intended to be used, it will all come together and make total sense to you. Plus, using these worksheets will transform your life. In this edition of the book, I've deliberately added more reader comments regarding the different worksheets to share their enthusiasm and provide encouragement as you get started.

One way to think of each of these two worksheets is literally to read the titles backwards:

- The **Monthly Budget Worksheet** is really a practice *Worksheet* to outline some kind of a beginning *Budget* for the next *Month* so you are better prepared. The numbers may not be exact, and you may not be sure what you will really be spending, but this will give you a starting point to work from.

- The **Monthly Expense Record** is a real *Record* of your spending. You will use this worksheet to *Record* every *Expense* you incur every day of the *Month.* This is how you will know how much you truly spent for the entire month.

Then the next month, when you are preparing again for the upcoming month (using the **Monthly Budget Worksheet**), you may have a few more realistic expense numbers (which you didn't have before) to use as you plan for upcoming expenses. The best examples of where having more realistic figures really helps tend to be groceries, meals out, and recreation/entertainment. In the beginning, when my clients express total confusion regarding these categories, I encourage them to guess. Then they are often more motivated to start recording these expenses so they have a better idea of what they actually spend.

Consider Lao-tzu's quote: "A journey of a thousand miles begins with a single step." For now, I suggest taking that first step on this financial journey and practicing with these worksheets one step at a time.

"I would be lost without my workbook. It's my bible. By keeping it next to the coffee and kids' money for school, the workbook is always handy. I color-code expenses for my kids, and under pets I highlight the expenses of the horses in yellow and dogs in red so I know the real cost of each."

Yearly Budget Worksheet
(Non-Monthly Anticipated Expenses)

"I just wanted to let you know how much your book changed the way I look at our money. In particular, the Yearly Budget made a HUGE impact on my thinking. It is amazing how much the yearly expenses can increase your overall expenses. Planning these expenses out in advance makes such a difference."

—Jennifer M., FL

Why a Yearly Budget Worksheet?

This worksheet is designed to give you a general yearly overview of your non-recurring *irregular, occasional, non-monthly,* and *periodic* expenses at a glance. This method often provides a more manageable approach than the use of files, notes on the calendar, or even some software programs.

Having this information can prevent those pay periods when you finally have all the bills paid and give a sigh of relief only to be deluged the next day with quarterly HOA dues or property tax bills you had overlooked or not anticipated, which put your whole budget in a tailspin once again.

By having all this information *written down* as early in the year as possible, you can use it to make necessary arrangements ahead of time. How much money should you put aside in your reserve savings account for the dental work, could you postpone that new sofa, how can the vacation be less costly, is it time to cut back on the gifts? By thinking these options through ahead of time and taking action, you won't be falling back on the credit cards or loans to get you through the year and getting back into debt.

"For us the Yearly Budget Worksheet was key and filled out first. We have so many expenses that pop up at different times of the year, and I had already been dividing up our savings account into separate mini-accounts to keep track of how much was saved for taxes, vacation money, etc.... By tying the Yearly Budget Worksheet in with the monthly budget and monthly expense worksheets, we were able to get a better idea of our spending this month. This was important,

since we just started contributing to my husband's 401(k) and therefore had less income this month with the pretax deduction."

—Christine R., NH

Filling in Your Yearly Budget Worksheet

Be patient as you go through this first worksheet, the **Yearly Budget Worksheet**, on page 53. It will require more time initially. However, the insights and information you gain will be well worth your time. *Once this worksheet is completed, it becomes a valuable reference page for the remainder of the year.*

To get started, grab your pencil, eraser, and calculator, or open your purchased Excel Budget Kit spreadsheets. Then gather up your checkbook registers or bank statements, insurance papers, credit card statements, and any other related household papers that may give the exact or estimated *amounts* of expenses plus the *months* these expenses are due or paid.

Start at the top left on page 53. Look at the expense category list on the left. If an expense applies to you, move across the page to the right and fill in the exact or estimated amount under the month or months the expense is due. I suggest pencil initially because as you work this through, changes and new additions will definitely come up.

See the **Suggestion List** on page 51 at the end of these instructions to find additional and often overlooked expenses that may apply to your household but are not on this worksheet. The worksheet is deliberately kept generic so you can adjust it to your own unique needs.

For those expense categories where you really don't have a clue what the cost will be, guess. That's right, just enter some amount. It is okay not to be perfect and it is also more valuable to keep moving through this exercise than to use the missing information as a reason to stop or get discouraged. You are already going through the most important process by thinking about these expenses and filling in most of the information. You can always edit information or add to this section later as new or more accurate information becomes available.

Additional Notes about the Categories

This worksheet is a guideline for you. You may find you have to add or cross out and replace certain categories. Remember to do whatever works best for your unique financial picture.

This section will be especially helpful if you are on a very tight budget this year. Some of your expenses like insurance or taxes will be fixed, and there will be no room for negotiating or eliminating this expense.

On the other hand, a number of the expenses may not be so immediate, and they may not even be considered "needs," but they are still preferred when the extra money is available. When you have the whole picture in front of you and see the total cost, it will be easier to make decisions about how to handle those expenses when the money is still tight.

Be sure to review the **Suggestion List** following these instructions so you can fully take advantage of this worksheet and include all the valuable information that belongs here. Below are a few notes for some of the categories.

Home/Yard Maintenance. This can include expenses that range from a new mattress to an addition to the house or backyard. If you have been thinking about new furniture and have been trying to decide when you can afford it, use this **Yearly Budget Worksheet** for your planning.

Auto Expenses. If you stop to think this area through ahead of time, you can estimate when you might need tires or need to take your car in for its 60,000-mile checkup. This would also naturally include regular quarterly oil changes.

Health Expenses. These are often difficult to know in advance, yet it is helpful to think about the different areas on the **Suggestion List** ahead of time so you can *anticipate* a possible expense rather than *react* to it. Put some estimate down, even the small co-pays, to remind you of the expenses throughout the year.

Vacations. Plan your vacations in advance. Keep in mind the mini-weekend trip as well as those holiday family visits and summer vacations. Both gifts and vacations are good practice places for learning to live within your income. You may enjoy buying expensive gifts or going on exotic vacations, but if this puts a hardship on your budget, you may have to reevaluate your priorities. Either spend less on these categories or less on some other categories.

Gifts. For some households, these are a minimal expense. Yet for others who place a high priority on gifts, this can be a major expense and budget buster when remembering the gifts as well as the party expenses for: Christmas, birthdays, weddings, Mother's and Father's Days, anniversaries, baby showers, graduation, etc. Planning out all this information ahead of time will make it all more manageable.

The **Gift Giving Worksheet** on page 56 is a separate worksheet to use for outlining all the gifts you plan to give *throughout* the year. You can total the amounts for each month and transfer those totals to the "Gift" category on the **Yearly Budget Worksheet**. Even though Christmas gifts are often purchased throughout the year, I do suggest putting the whole Christmas gift expense total under December (unless you know the months you will make these early purchases), only to keep this planning simple.

Holiday Events. This expense will vary from household to household depending on how you celebrate Valentine's Day, July 4th, Halloween, Thanksgiving, and other traditional and religious events in your family. Don't forget the cost of decorating the house or purchasing a new Halloween costume along with all the other related expenses. By listing these estimates as well as the others on this page, you will have a more realistic approach to all your upcoming expenses.

The **Christmas/Holiday Expense Worksheet** on page 58 can help you fine-tune the real expense of the Christmas and holiday season on top of the gift expense. Many of my clients will guess an amount for this category. Then when we work through the details of the real estimate with the worksheet, the total amount is usually three times their guess.

"I started using your book when it got to the point where we just didn't know where all the money was going. I figured most of it was going to meals out, which turned out to be true, but what shocked me was the amount being spent on gifts!"

—Joan R., CT

All of these various expenses are just more examples of "where the money goes."

How to Use this Information

Once you have taken time to estimate and project your upcoming non-monthly expenses, you have valuable information that graphically shows you which months will be light and which ones will be difficult to deal with. At this point, you can evaluate each expense and consider your choices: you can cut back, postpone, modify, or eliminate the expense. Which choice best fits your personal needs?

When you total all of these expenses, you can quickly see why there never seems to be enough money. This is where the Reserve Savings Account mentioned earlier in the "How to Use *The Budget Kit*" section now makes more sense. When you total these expenses and divide by 12 (to get your monthly average), you can see how much money must be put aside each month to prepare for these upcoming expenses. You then can transfer this amount onto the **Monthly Budget Worksheet** and list it as "Reserve Savings" to help you plan ahead for the month.

As you look at this completed worksheet, what does it tell you? First, as mentioned above, you can see which months are going to be high-stress months and which ones will be manageable light months. Now you have a guideline to let you know which month would be better for taking on additional expenses.

Second, you can see what you ideally need to put aside each month to save for all these expenses. If that amount is too much at this time, pick some of the fixed and most expensive categories, like property tax, gifts, auto repairs, etc., and start putting aside one-twelfth of those totals. You can also use the **Goals Saving Record** in Part One on page 36 or the general **Savings Activity Record** in Part Three on page 180 to help track your savings.

Third, and most significantly, that monthly average amount is having a huge *indirect* impact on your regular monthly budget, but you don't always realize this, because it's not showing up directly. Consequently, *this impact usually shows up in the form of added credit card debt, new home equity line of credit, more or larger loans, financial juggling, doing without, and overall frustration.* It's like a computer program running *silently* in the background.

Now that you can recognize this and realize what has been happening to your overall budget each year, you can do something about it. That's the exciting part. As one woman said, "I'm depressed and excited at the same time!"

Consider customizing this worksheet by using color highlighters or color pens to separate children's expenses, solo-prenuer business expenses, or other categories that pertain to your situation. Some small business owners use the very bottom portion to outline all the periodic business expenses.

Reminder

This worksheet is your guideline and is meant to be as flexible as possible. You are the one who decides how to utilize the worksheet and the information to your best advantage.

> *"Even though I now use another program, I still use your Yearly Budget Worksheet to take a look at how much of our monthly income should be allocated to our monthly budget to cover those irregular expenses. I review this quarterly to make sure that we're on track with the expenses that we can reasonably plan for. We also now have a nicely padded emergency fund for the surprises. In addition, by following a budget, we have eliminated all debt except for home-related debt and have been able to make extra payments to shorten these loans as well.*
>
> *"I hope that you are still influencing lots of other families to start taking charge of their finances by walking them through the steps to create their first budget."*
>
> —Christine R., NH

THE ONLINE/ELECTRONIC CONNECTION TO *THE BUDGET KIT*

Online Bill Payments

You can coordinate all of the information you gathered and listed for this **Yearly Budget Worksheet** with any online bill payment service you use (your bank's website or the website of the company itself). On the website, go to the "Payee List" and add the names (and all required information) of the companies or individuals you will be paying on a non-monthly, periodic basis throughout the year.

If you know the exact amount and date due for a particular expense, you can schedule it to be paid automatically. If you prefer to initiate the payment amount and date yourself, just add that final information when you know the funds are available to make the payment. Remember, allow at least five business days before the due date with all online bill payments.

Just like reviewing the **Yearly Budget Worksheet** on page 53, at the beginning of each month, you will visually be reminded of the bill and amount due whenever you pull up your "Pending Payments List." You can also arrange email or text alerts. These are great reminders for you to be prepared and make arrangements for upcoming expenses.

Online Budget Programs

Depending on the program you are using, you may be able to utilize this same concept and plan ahead for your periodic, non-monthly expenses electronically. Try to set up the program to automatically set aside one-twelfth of the total periodic expenses into savings each month. Perhaps it will be easier to do the **Yearly Budget Worksheet** manually and then just plug in that monthly amount needed for savings. Or there may be a tool on the program you are using that will do this automatically after you set up your periodic expenses.

SUGGESTION LIST—ADDITIONAL NON-MONTHLY EXPENSES

You can either complete this information here and then transfer it to the **Yearly Budget Worksheet** or use this as your guideline as you fill in the worksheet directly from these ideas.

Some of the expenses listed may be a monthly expense for you. If so, enter those expenses on the **Monthly Budget Worksheet**, *not here*. The focus of the **Yearly Budget Worksheet** is only on the *periodic, quarterly, semiannual, annual, and non-monthly* expenses to help you remember and anticipate them ahead of time.

	Description	Amount(s)	Months Due
Housing	Property Taxes		
	Homeowners Insurance/Renter's Insurance		
	Association/Condo Dues		
	Storage/Garage/PO Box		
	Yard/Garden Supplies/Equipment Repair		
	Yard Service/Maintenance		
	Pool Chemicals/Maintenance		
	Pest/Termite Control		
	Security System		
	Home Improvement Projects		
	Home Repairs/Maintenance		
	Carpet Cleaning/Window Cleaning		
	Dry Cleaning (drapes, bedding)		
	Home Furnishings/Decorating		
	Furniture/Appliances/Electronic Equipment		
	Maintenance Agreements		
	Other _____		
Utilities (Non-Monthly)	Fuel/Propane		
	Firewood		
	Waste Management/Dumping Fees		
	Water/Water Softener		
	Other _____		
Transportation	Vehicle #1 Insurance		
	Vehicle #2 Insurance		
	Boat/RV/Motorcycle Insurance & Expenses		
	Emission Inspection		
	License Renewal/Registration		
	Oil Change/Tune-Up		
	Other Maintenance and Repairs		
	Other _____		
Health	Other Insurance		
	Medical Exams/Lab Tests		
	Visits (sick kids, allergy, etc.)		
	Physical Exam/School Physical		
	Prescriptions		
	Chiropractor		
	Dermatologist		
	Dental Exams/X-Rays/Cleanings		
	Dental Work Needed		
	Orthodontia		
	Vision Exam/Glasses/Contacts		
	Alternative Health Practitioners		
	Vitamins/Supplements/Homeopathic		
	Other _____		
Insurance (Other)	Life/Umbrella Insurance		
	Disability/Long-Term Care Insurance		
	Other _____		

	Description	Amount(s)	Months Due
Memberships	Church/Temple	_____	_____
	Country Club	_____	_____
	Credit Card Annual Fees	_____	_____
	Gym Annual Fees	_____	_____
	Organizations/Clubs	_____	_____
	Professional Dues/License	_____	_____
	Auto Club	_____	_____
	Sports	_____	_____
	Warehouse Clubs	_____	_____
	Other _____	_____	_____
Computer/ Electronics	Hardware/Software/Apps	_____	_____
	Upgrades/Printer Supplies	_____	_____
	Service/Maintenance	_____	_____
	Classes/Training/Assistance	_____	_____
Education (Adult)	Tuition	_____	_____
	Book/Supply Expenses	_____	_____
	Trade Journals/Magazines/Newspapers	_____	_____
	Workshops/Seminars/Speakers	_____	_____
	Other _____	_____	_____
Clothing (Adults and Children)	Work Clothes/Uniforms/Shoes	_____	_____
	Seasonal Clothes/Shoes/Jackets	_____	_____
	Sports Clothes/Special Events	_____	_____
	Dry Cleaning/Alterations/Shoe Repair	_____	_____
Recreation (Adults)	Parties	_____	_____
	Concerts/Sports Events/Season Tickets	_____	_____
	Fees: Permits/Tournament/League	_____	_____
	Hobbies/Sports Equipment/Lessons	_____	_____
	Boat/Plane Storage	_____	_____
	Other _____	_____	_____
Vacation/Trips	Transportation	_____	_____
	Lodging/Meals/Snacks	_____	_____
	Sights/Activities/Theater/Galleries	_____	_____
	Shopping/Souvenirs/Film & Processing	_____	_____
Children/ Elder Care	Tuition/College Expenses	_____	_____
	School Supplies/Tutors/Uniform	_____	_____
	Photos/Yearbooks/Class Ring/Letter Jacket	_____	_____
	Prom/Homecoming (flowers, hair, dinner, etc.)	_____	_____
	Field Trips/Contests/Expos/Fund-Raising/Fairs	_____	_____
	Camp Registration/Supplies	_____	_____
	Sports Equip./Fees/Clinics/Season End	_____	_____
	Music Lessons/Equipment/Recitals/Costumes	_____	_____
	Nursing Home/Health Aide	_____	_____
	Other _____	_____	_____
Pets	Pet Food/Toys	_____	_____
	Grooming/Pet Hotel/Day Care/Sitter	_____	_____
	Vet Expense/Shots/Rx/Dental/Other	_____	_____
	Training/License	_____	_____
Misc.	Donations/Contributions	_____	_____
	Tax Preparation	_____	_____
	Taxes Due/Estimated Taxes	_____	_____
	Retirement Savings (IRA)	_____	_____

YEARLY BUDGET WORKSHEET

(Non-Monthly Anticipated Expenses)

FIXED AND ESTIMATED NON-MONTHLY EXPENSES

		JAN.	FEB.	MAR.	APR.	MAY	JUNE	JULY	AUG.	SEPT.	OCT.	NOV.	DEC.	TOTAL	MO. AVG.
Housing	Property Tax				550							550		$ 1,100	$ 92
	Homeowners Insurance													$ —	$ —
	Home/Yard Maintenance				Yard 200			Carpets 250						$ 450	$ 38
	Utilities *Garbage*		65			65				65			65	$ 260	$ 22
Transportation	Auto Insurance	Van Car		500 425						500 425				$ 1,000 $ 850	$ 154
	Auto Expenses		Lube 30	Tires 250		Lube 30			Lube 30	Lic. 100		Tune-up 250		$ 690	$ 58
Health	Insurance—Other	Umbrella	415											$ 415	$ 35
	Medical Expenses	Rx 75		250		Dr. A 30			Rx 75			Lab 70		$ 500	$ 42
	Dental/Vision Expenses		Dental 750				Vision 300		Dental 75					$ 1,125	$ 94
Additional Non-Monthly Expenses	Dues/Fees *Taxes*		Prof. Lic. 125		Tax Prep 300		Ent. Bk 35	AAA 35				Gym 55		$ 550	$ 46
	Education/Tuition			Seminar 150						Seminar 100				$ 250	$ 21
	Clothing *Child*	Shoes/Coat 320				350			450					$ 1,120	$ 93
	Recreation					Fish Lic. 35	60		75					$ 170	$ 14
	Vacation/Trips						1,500					300		$ 1,800	$ 150
	Magazines		YM 16			Kip 20							BL 39	$ 75	$ 6
	Gifts—Birthday	25	15	50			15	100			100	75		$ 380	$ 32
	Gifts—Other	Anniv. 40				Grad. 75	F. Day 30		Shower 35		Wedding 50		Xmas 900	$ 1,130	$ 94
	Holiday Events							40			Halloween 60	TG 70	Xmas 400	$ 570	$ 48
	Children's Activities				Field Trip 50		Camp 250	Lessons 65	65	School 75	Photos 75			$ 580	$ 48
	Pets													$ —	$ —
	Donations	15		WWF 25				G.P. 30			RC 50	CRS 100		$ 220	$ 28
	Personal				25					Spa 80	25			$ 130	$ 11
	Total	475	1,351	1,715	1,125	540	2,195	580	730	1,320	460	1,370	1,504	$13,365	$1,114

Reserve Savings: Total Expenses $ _____13,365_____ **divided by 12 = $** _____1,114_____ **/Month** (Rounded Up)

YEARLY BUDGET WORKSHEET

(Non-Monthly Anticipated Expenses)

FIXED AND ESTIMATED NON-MONTHLY EXPENSES

		JAN.	FEB.	MAR.	APR.	MAY	JUNE	JULY	AUG.	SEPT.	OCT.	NOV.	DEC.	TOTAL	MO. AVG.
Housing	Property Tax														
	Homeowners Insurance														
	Home/Yard Maintenance														
	Utilities														
Transportation	Auto Insurance														
	Auto Expenses														
Health	Insurance— Other														
	Medical Expenses														
	Dental/Vision Expenses														
Additional Non-Monthly Expenses	Dues/Fees														
	Education/ Tuition														
	Clothing														
	Recreation														
	Vacation/Trips														
	Gifts—Birthday														
	Gifts—Other														
	Holiday Events														
	Children's Activities														
	Pets														
	Total														

Reserve Savings: Total Expenses $ _____   divided by 12 = $ _____ / Month

Gift Giving Worksheet

Gift giving is often one of the most underestimated and overlooked budget categories in many households. People are often amazed, once they start recording all their expenses, just how much money is actually spent on gifts. It is not uncommon to forget occasional events or extended family members or teachers, bosses, hairdressers, and pets on this gift list when trying to estimate the overall gift budget.

This **Gift Giving Worksheet** works as a reminder of often forgotten expenses as you anticipate the total yearly cost for all upcoming events involving gifts. Remembering Christmas and birthdays is generally easy. Events such as Father's Day or your parents' anniversary, however, are often overlooked until the month they occur. Even if you don't buy gifts but send flowers or go out to dinner instead, include these costs in your plan. By making an outline of all the members of your family and your friends and all the events celebrated in your household on this worksheet, and how much you want to budget for each, you will have a handy total picture of what gift expenses to expect. You then can transfer these amounts to the "Gifts" section of the **Yearly Budget Worksheet** under the appropriate months.

As you think of gift ideas, you could add them in small print to this worksheet as well.

GIFT GIVING WORKSHEET

	Name	Amount: Christmas/ Hanukkah	Amount: Birthday	Actual Month Due	Other Events Happening*	Amount: Other Events	Actual Month Due
Spouse		$	$			$	
Parents/Self							
Children/Grandchildren							
Sisters/Brothers							
Grandparents							

*Other: Anniversaries, weddings, showers, babies, Mother's Day, Father's Day, graduations, Bar/Bat Mitzvahs, religious events

GIFT GIVING WORKSHEET

	Name	Amount: Christmas/ Hanukkah	Amount: Birthday	Actual Month Due	Other Events Happening*	Amount: Other Events	Actual Month Due
Aunts/Uncles		$	$			$	
Nieces/Nephews							
Friends/Work/Other							
Children's Friends							
	Total of both pages	$	$			$	

*Other: Anniversaries, weddings, showers, babies, Mother's Day, Father's Day, graduations, Bar/Bat Mitzvahs, religious events

CHRISTMAS/HOLIDAY EXPENSE WORKSHEET

Item	Estimate	Already Have	Actual Cost
Tree/Wreath			
Lights—House/Tree			
Baked Goods/Gingerbread House			
Parties/Food/Liquor/Beverages/Host Gifts			
Poinsettias/Candles/Decorations/Crafts			
Gift Wrap/Greeting Cards			
Postage/Shipping/Boxes			
Digital Photo Processing/Family Portraits			
Clothes/Shoes/Jewelry			
Meals Out			
Movies/Ballet/Plays/Galleries/Travel/Tour			
Workplace Events			
Donations			
Batteries/Misc. (for gifts) Other			
Total Amount			

SOURCE OF MONEY FOR GIFTS AND HOLIDAY EXPENSES

Amount Needed

Total Amount for Gifts:
  (See Gift Giving Worksheet) $ _____

Total Amount—Holiday Expenses:
  (See worksheet above) $ _____

TOTAL AMOUNT NEEDED
  for Gifts and Holiday Expenses: $ _____

List how much is available from the following sources to cover these holiday expenses:

Total Amount Available		
Source	**Amount**	**Notes**
Current Income		
Overtime/Part-Time Job		
Savings Account(s)		
Gift Money/Bonus		
Total Amount Available to Cover Expenses		
Total Amount Needed for Gifts & Holiday Expenses		
Amount Short/Extra*		

*Total amount needed − Total amount available to cover expenses = Amount short or extra

Outline a plan for covering amount that is short for holiday expenses:

Source	**Amount**	**Notes**
Overtime/Part-Time Job		
Charge on Credit Cards		
Borrow		
Other		
Total Amount Need to Borrow		

Monthly Budget Worksheet

Why a Monthly Budget Worksheet?

The **Monthly Budget Worksheet** is designed to provide a guideline for coordinating your monthly bills and expenses with your *take-home* pay. Your monthly bills are often easier to remember because most bills come in the mail or through email. Forgotten, however, are the expenses each month such as meals eaten out, haircuts, gifts, books, DVDs, seminars, and the like that often throw off the monthly budget.

This worksheet is especially helpful during those lean times when your income is reduced and the amount of bills to pay exceeds the money coming in. This guideline will give you a better overall picture of your monthly obligations and lifestyle expenses. The categories are kept general to allow for flexibility and necessary additions based on your own personal financial needs.

Often something as simple as this worksheet can be the difference between financial chaos and financial control. For the Mathews, the true test came when the commission check was exceptionally low one month. After months of working diligently on their budget, this young, ambitious couple had the skills and tools to tighten up and be creative about their spending. They knew what to do. Banana bread was made at home to replace the sales meeting bagels, all meals out were eliminated, brown bag meals and soggy sandwiches replaced the business meals out while on the road, and all other discretionary spending was cut back. By the end of the month, the Mathews were ecstatic as they made it through the month financially intact—all the bills were paid, good meals were eaten at home, no credit card charges, no little loans, and best of all, they felt totally motivated by their ability to take control of the situation.

How to Get Started

To use the **Monthly Budget Worksheet**, look at the filled in sample on page 69 and follow these instructions. Start with the top row next to "Income Source" and indicate in each column where your money is coming from for that month, whether it is from your job, your spouse's job, your checkbook balance rolled over from the previous month, investment or rental income, savings, child or spousal support, a refund, trust funds, Internet sales, Social Security, and so on.

Next, on the second row next to "Net Income Total Amount" ①, write down the *net amount* of each paycheck or source of other money that will be used to pay for those monthly expenses. How many columns you fill in depends on how often you are paid each month. Of course, there are many job situations where the amount may vary or is not always known, such as with commission sales. If this is the case, make a very *conservative* estimate until the actual amount is known. If your income is very erratic, you can also work with the **Variable Income Worksheet** on page 89.

You will notice the emphasis on net income and not on gross income throughout the workbook. This way, you are dealing only with the cash you actually have for paying your bills. Your payroll deductions and taxes are not being ignored. You can record that information on the **End-of-the-Year Tax Information** worksheet on page 155.

On the third row under the "Income Source" amount, there is room to add the date ② each paycheck is received. This will help with your planning when working around due dates and paying your bills.

Finally, total all of the income and other sources of money across the top row and enter that total amount in the box at the bottom left corner of the page right next to "Total Income." ⑤

Handling and Applying the Reserve Savings Account

The sample on page 69 shows an added income of "Reserve Savings" on the top right. Even though this money from your Reserve Savings Account is not actually income, the amount of money withdrawn from your savings to cover the periodic expenses is listed there to show you how the concept works.

In this example, the $1,320 figure comes from the total of all expenses with astericks under the "Amount" column. If you look back on the **Yearly Budget Worksheet**, on the bottom you will notice that the total for September is $1,320. Ideally, if you have $1,320 in your Reserve Savings Account, you can use that reserve money to cover these periodic expenses for that month. This way, you are not interfering with your monthly budget for your regular planned expenses.

Now stay with me here. If you jumped ahead, you already noticed under the Fixed Amounts expenses the Reserve Savings of $1,114. This is the monthly average from the **Yearly Budget Worksheet** that was designated for savings to help you build up a reserve and be prepared for these varying periodic non-monthly expenses.

The reason I've listed both the full amounts of the Reserve Savings of $1,320 as income and the $1,114 as a fixed expense under Fixed Amounts/ Reserve Savings is to help you understand the concept of having a basic flow of money in and out.

Could you just apply the $1,114 toward the $1,320 worth of expenses and not bother to deposit that money? Of course you could. Just remember, you still wouldn't have enough to cover all the $1,320 worth of periodic expenses for that month and would need to withdraw the difference. If you chose this second approach, the income figure under Reserve Savings would only be the difference of $206 ($1,320 for September actual expenses minus $1,114 monthly Reserve Savings).

What Makes This Worksheet Unique

Actually, the process discussed above is one of the unique features of the **Monthy Budget Worksheet**. It was designed to help you comprehend how to blend all those different financial facets of your personal lifestyle and budget. Many of my clients initially express their concern and confusion over how to pull everything together financially and to see all the information in one place. Using the overall approach described in this section to create a monthly budget often helps clarify the process.

Now let's look at all those bills. List every bill and expense you can think of that will be coming up for that particular month in the second column called "Amount."③ Included will be the obvious, regular monthly bills as well as the incidental, like planning to buy a new suit, attending a workshop, or having someone service your computer that month. This is not necessarily an *average* monthly budget that is being developed. And although it may well turn out to be an average monthly budget, the real purpose here is to take time to outline the specific month coming up and look at all of its unique variable expenses beyond the average amounts. For example, if your relatives are coming to visit for a week next month, your grocery, meals out, utility, gasoline, and entertainment amounts may all be higher than usual that month.

This proactive planning approach is what makes this budgeting process more powerful than the standard method of taking the yearly total of expenses and dividing it by 12 months for a monthly average.

The other unique feature is learning how to coordinate the timing of the income with the due dates and needs of the expenses using this worksheet. I have had numerous clients finally "get it" when they saw how to work the payments and general expenses according to the timing of the income. *They no longer had to try to pay all their bills with the first paycheck out of fear of running out of money and then figure out how to live the next few weeks with limited money until they were paid again.*

Other clients used this worksheet to determine ahead of time how much cash to pull out for each week for various cash expenses and eliminated all the incidental nonplanned runs to the ATM machine.

This worksheet will definitely help you become proactive and more relaxed in your approach to managing money instead of staying in a reactive mode.

So now let's review how to fill in the expenses in the column under the "Amount" heading. The sample on page 69 will help you get a better idea.

Pay Yourself First

Notice that "Allowance/Mad Money" and "Savings" are under "Fixed Amounts." ④ The phrase "pay yourself first" has been said many times. It is a valid statement that applies to savings as well as to your basic personal needs. If you penny-pinch to the point where there is no money left for "Allowance/Mad Money," you will end up bickering, frustrated, and disappointed with the whole budget idea. The "Allowance/Mad Money" should be yours to do with as you please. Decide how much "Allowance/Mad Money" each member needs in order to allow for little splurges and yet not ignore the necessary expenses.

Just as important under "Fixed Amounts" is "Savings." Again, this is paying yourself first. Consider "Savings" as an *expense*, setting aside a specific amount or percentage of your check at the same time you are completing the other categories of the worksheet. In this manner, you will be thinking of "Savings" as an expense so that it is planned for regularly and not dependent on leftover funds.

Remember the different savings accounts—reserve (for upcoming known bills and expenses listed on the **Yearly Budget Worksheet**), emergency (equivalent to *at least three months* of take-home pay for unknown disasters), and goals (wish list)—and try to save regularly for them. See the **Savings Activity Record** on page 180 for tracking your savings.

Once you have saved enough money for the reserve and emergency accounts, you will realize that it is actually possible to save money. Saving for your goals soon becomes more exciting and challenging as you realize that reaching your goals is now possible.

Now for Some Practice at Budgeting

In many cases, such as utilities or other areas under the "Fixed Variable" and "Occasional" headings on the left side, the exact amount of the bill is unknown. For those categories, this is where your budgeting practice comes in as you estimate the bills until the exact amount is known. Remember to keep in mind those other expenses that are not seen as bills but show up on a pretty regular basis: groceries, gas, entertainment, prescriptions, and so on. Those must be planned for as well. Here you will take an estimated guess (budget) as to what you will need and the amount you can spend. If you use the **Monthly Expense Record** starting on page 126 for tracking your expenses each month, you will have a better sense of some averages to use for these categories when estimating. Once you become familiar with estimating your expenditures, you will successfully begin to live within your budget. If your budget is realistic, you will soon choose to eliminate certain unnecessary items to remain within the projected budget.

More Month Than Money—Now What?

Before you total the "Amount" column, think again if there is anything else that may be coming up as an expense for the particular month you are outlining. Look at the categories on the **Monthly Expense Record** and the **Suggestion List—Additional Non-Monthly Expenses** in the Yearly Budget Worksheet section and see if any ideas are triggered for possible expenses. And finally, look at the **Yearly Budget Worksheet**. If you have not put the one-twelfth into reserve savings, did you still include those unique expenses listed when planning for this particular month?

Now it's time to tally up and face the total. Put that total figure for this "Amount" column at the bottom next to "Total Expenses." ⑤ As you filled in this column, you probably were already telling yourself this is more than you have coming in. If that is the case, at least now you can see it in black and white and know why some of the months have been running short and why those expenses probably ended up on the credit cards.

Remember, *this worksheet is done before the month ever begins*. It is a projection of your anticipated budget for the next month coming up. That means you now have the time and opportunity to take charge and do something about this information. You always have the following choices: postpone, cut back, eliminate, or find creative alternatives.

Contact the creditors and see what special arrangements you can make. Many will accommodate you and allow postponed or partial payments if you notify them. What can you eliminate? Lattes, books, CDs, meals out, full-price movies, clothes, and gadgets are starters. Go through and reevaluate each expense.

What else can you do? How can you bring more money in? Can you get more overtime hours or a part-time job? Do you have enough "stuff" to have a yard sale? What if you took your unused books, CDs, clothes, furniture, electronic gadgets, and games to the resale shops or sold them online for some extra cash?

In the meantime, possibly you have been building a small emergency fund and can cover part or all of the expenses this time by withdrawing the necessary amount. This should be an absolute last resort, however, with cutbacks planned for the next few months so that you can replenish your emergency fund once again.

Timing Income with Payments and Expenses

This part of the worksheet is designed primarily to give you a planning guide for coordinating the timing of your income with the due dates of your bills and expenses. This prepares you ahead of time to know just how much you will have available at different times of the month for different expenses.

Now that you have reworked your numbers so your expenses match your income, go back to the top of the "Amount" column in the "Fixed Amounts" section. Distribute and balance the more expensive bills over the different pay periods in each column. Fill in the amounts, *based on due dates and income dates*. If some pay periods, like the beginning of the month, are pretty top heavy with bills, try contacting the creditor and see about arranging to change the date according to your next paycheck for future payments.

Another method is to allocate small portions from some or all of the paychecks to cover a large bill, such as the mortgage. What some readers have done in those cases is to itemize a portion under different pay periods and then write a check for that amount and keep it in the envelope until the final check and full amount is ready. They then sent the envelope with the multiple checks totaling the complete payment.

As you review the sample on page 69, notice the disbursement of expenses throughout the columns of this worksheet. Some amounts, like "Car Payment," are distributed under one income column and handled in full. Other categories, like groceries, gasoline, and meals out, for example, have the amounts divided across the various income columns and when added up *total* the "Amount" to the left.

Also, at the bottom under "Total Excess" and "Total Short," you see how closely the "Total Expense" and "Total Income" match. This is where most of your time and work will come in, when doing this manually, as you fine-tune the numbers to balance each of the "Income" columns with the expenses as closely as you can. You will definitely want to *work with pencil* as you fine-tune these numbers.

Again, this is a guideline, not an exercise in exact bookkeeping. As you will see on the bottom of the sample, there are some periods with some excess amounts and some with shortfalls. But throughout the month, using this guideline for planning will help you stay mindful of your spending, keep you from running short some weeks, and prevent the all-too-familiar experience of "more month than money."

Customizing the Income Columns for Your Household

It is always fascinating to learn the different ways clients and readers have found to utilize the full functionality of this worksheet. Listed below are a few ways to adapt this worksheet, primarily the use of the "Income" columns, so it works best for your household and financial situation.

Checking Account Balance

Since most households roll over to the next month with some balance in the checking account before the next paycheck arrives, it often makes sense to use the first column and designate it "Checking Balance." This amount is the money available to handle the most immediate expense needs the first week of the month.

Again, be resourceful with this layout. If you need another column for an additional paycheck, you can create another column, use the outside border space, or combine the amount of the first early paycheck in the month with the checking balance.

As with all of these worksheets, find creative ways to make them work for you, including to help work out ways to set up your software more effectively.

Credit Card Use

There are two aspects to this approach. The first addresses the deliberate and conscious use of the credit card by putting the majority of major expenses on the credit card and always paying off the balance. This leverages the card mileage and other benefits, offers the convenience of paying one check for all the expenses (and paying off the credit card in full), and having most of the spending records on one statement. Therefore, as an example, the second column labeled "Kim" can be designated instead as "Credit Card," and all the expenses under the "Amount" column that are paid with the credit card are then also listed under this "Credit Card" column.

The second aspect of this approach is using the credit card as "supplemental income." It is important to recognize this practice for what it is and understand that you are truly using the credit card for your "supplemental income" and technically borrowing money to get through the month. The goal, obviously, is to get to the point where you are balancing your income and your spending and not continuing with this risky practice too long. In the meantime, the way to use this **Monthly Budget Worksheet** proactively to best understand and to stay conscious of what you are doing through this whole exercise is to use one column designated for credit card use only. This helps you to identify which critical expenses will have to fall on the credit card this particular month in order to make it through the month intact. This solution is used only after all other adjustments and arrangements are handled in the initial planning discussed earlier, and there is still a shortage for the month. Ideally, when you plan out the following month, you will be sure to find a way to add more to your payment for your credit card expense.

Reimbursements

Dealing with business reimbursements for your job in some cases can get a little crazy and confusing depending on timing and actual amounts reimbursed. Since all of these situations are so variable, find a way to make this work best for your situation. Create a column designated for the anticipated amount of the reimbursement for the month you are planning. List what your total expense needs are going to be for the current upcoming month you are planning under the "Amount" column. You then have a way to show how some or all of those expenses can be covered with the previous reimbursement check coming in for the current month and keep that business expense category more separated in the household budget.

Bonus—Overtime—Gift Money

During those months you happen to have extra money from a variety of sources, designate one of the income columns with this title and then determine how you will prioritize and best use this money for the expenses during the month you are planning. Perhaps a big chunk will be added in the savings section. In this case, you would be sure to list the amount of savings as one of your "Expenses" under the "Amount" column and then show that amount again on the column you designate as "Bonus." Or you may add an additional amount to the credit card payment and show part of the payment from your usual paycheck and then a second payment from this bonus money.

For more ideas on how to best distribute your bonus money with a plan rather than react to all the spending temptations, be sure to see the **Windfall Planner** on page 94 before making any decisions.

Cash

If you're having a hard time determining how much cash you need each month and how you will use cash only, designate one of the remaining columns as "Cash." When you finish outlining all of your expenses and coordinating the bills based on due dates, review the list and notice in which areas you tend to use mostly cash (lunches out, church donations, bottled water). Next, list each of these amounts under the "Cash" column. Be sure to put a dollar amount for this cash at the top on the "Net Income Total Amount" line/row. In this case, if the cash is coming from a paycheck, you will also need to be sure you subtracted that same amount from the net paycheck amount listed on the income column.

Getting Control of your Finances

You have just completed an important step in getting and keeping control of your finances. Of course, doing a **Monthly Budget Worksheet** does not change or increase the amount of actual money earned. *Being aware,* however, of where and how the money is spent will give you the feeling that you are beginning to control your money and will help you stretch the use of those dollars more than ever before.

Happy budgeting!

"I was shocked into action when I worked out my budget on the Monthly Budget Worksheet and realized I was $1,000 short. Now, after four years, all our bills are paid in full and we are completely out of debt. Without putting information down on paper every month, I don't think I could have done it."

THE ONLINE/ELECTRONIC CONNECTION TO *THE BUDGET KIT*

Online Bill Payments

This **Monthly Budget Worksheet** is actually an *ideal tool* to use if you are ready to simplify the bill payment process but prefer to continue using the hands-on system for outlining your monthly bills and expenses. Visually, you have everything down on one sheet and can easily see the amounts and dates for each of the bills.

To streamline the process of actually paying all those bills, you have a number of convenient cashless choices. You may already be using automatic bank withdrawals for utilities and loan payments on your home, cars, and other loans. Many people also choose to use their credit card for automatically paying fixed and regular monthly bills. They then pay the bill in full, enjoying the convenience and other benefits they receive by using a particular credit card.

Often, there are still payments due to small businesses and individuals who will only take checks. This is where online bill payment services through your bank or other service providers truly distinguish themselves. A majority of the services will pay any bill for you. Once you have signed up for the online bill pay service, all you have to do is enter the information for your new payee, indicate which account to use, how much to pay and when, and you are finished.

A final note if you aren't quite ready or don't trust paying your bills online. You can still take advantage of your online banking service. You can check your current balance and see what checks have cleared at anytime as you work out your plan with the **Monthly Budget Worksheet**. This may be the perfect way for you to slowly transition to online financial services.

Online Budget Programs

Most programs will have some method of setting up a budget for the month tied into the online bill payment service. Use this **Monthly Budget Worksheet** as a way to plan out your online program more comprehensively and as a reminder of all the categories of expenses to include for the month when setting up your budget online. Once all your information is in place and your various online financial accounts are set up, the system should automatically retrieve and set up all your spending and deposit records in one place. Whether you use credit cards, debit cards, ATMs, or checks, you should be able to assign each transaction to the correct category with just a click of your mouse or some transactions may assign automatically. Ideally, when everything is set up, this system will handle all your fixed, variable, and incidental bills seamlessly.

continued on next page

THE ONLINE/ELECTRONIC CONNECTION TO *THE BUDGET KIT* continued

Since most programs are going to help you see what you have spent and where you stand financially at any given time, it will still be up to you to outline a plan ahead of time that incorporates all of your upcoming monthly needs. You can use this **Monthly Budget Worksheet** as a guideline for determining the timing of your bills, based on your income and other money coming in to be sure your income carries you through the month. This worksheet will also help you outline ahead of time how much money you want to pull out for cash expenses.

Monthly Budget Worksheet on Excel

This is one of the core worksheets available on Excel and looks exactly the same on the screen as the worksheets in this book, with a separate tab on the bottom for every month. It is available at *http://moneytracker.com/books-TheBudgetKitExcel.htm* for a small extra fee. The true value of using Excel, beyond the quick calculations, is the ability to add and adjust the rows and columns more conveniently. Because of the variability in each household, there is usually more adjusting with the rows for the listed expenses or with the columns for the different income sources and planning systems. When readers and clients started using this worksheet, they noticed a dramatic difference in their planning and spending.

MONTHLY BUDGET WORKSHEET

(September)   **SAMPLE**

INCOME SOURCE:				Checking Bal.	Kim/Job	Chris/Job	Kim/Job	Reserve Savings
① Net Income Total Amount				$435	$1,707	$1,280	$1,707	$1,320

	Expenses	③ Amount	Date Due	Date Paid	Date ② Rcv.: 9/1	9/7	9/18	9/21	9/15
Fixed Amounts ④	Mortgage/Rent	984	5	2	984				
	Car Payments	291	10	5		291			
	Other Loans: Student	167	15	10		167			
	Internet Access	49	1	1	49				
	Day Care	—							
	Insurance SUV*	**500***	17	15					500
	Insurance Truck*	**425***	17	15					425
	Clubs/Dues	25	20	17				25	
	Savings—Emergency	100						100	
	Savings—Goals	65						65	
	Savings—Reserve	1,114			100	114	400	500	
	Allowance/Mad Money	50			50				
Fixed Variable	Electricity	75	20	18			75		
	Heating Oil/Gas	45	25	20			45		
	Water	35	11	8			35		
	Garbage*	**65***	18	15					65
	Telephone/Cell Phone	88	27	20			88		
	Cable TV/Satellite/TiVo	60	25	20			60		
	Groceries	550			100	150	100	200	
	Meals Out/School Lunch	195			70	55	25	45	
	Auto Expense/Gas	125			30	40		55	
	Auto—DMV*	**100***							100
	Child Allowance	40				20		20	
	Church/Charity	300				100		200	
Occasional	Household Supplies	100				20		80	
	Personal Hair*	**80***							80
	Clothes/Dry Cleaning	110			25	35		50	
	Medical Prescrip.	35				35			
	Child Expense School Exp.*	**75***							75
	Recreation Season Tickets*	**75***							75
	Counseling	130				65		65	
	Books, CDs, Movies, Videos	90				90			
Installment	Credit Cards:								
	Visa	100	25	16				100	
	MC	200	27	20				200	
Total ⑤	Total Income — See Note	$5,129			$435	$1,707	$1,280	$1,707	$1,320
	Total Expense Excludes *	$5,123			$424	$1,708	$1,286	$1,705	$1,320
	Total Excess	$6			$11			$2	
	Total Short					$–1	$–6		

Note: Total Income is from Income and Checking Balance only (*Excludes* Reserve Savings in right column).

* This Total Expense *excludes* all the expenses in bold with an * (see the far left column).

* Expenses in bold and with an * are paid from Reserve Savings (see the far right column) & not included in Total Expense.

This sample was laid out this way, excluding the expenses from Reserve Savings, to show how this concept works. The exact Totals would have $1,320 more in Income and $1,320 more in Expenses, balancing each other out.

MONTHLY BUDGET WORKSHEET

INCOME SOURCE:							
Net Income Total Amount							

	Expenses	Amount	Date Due	Date Paid	Date Rcv.:			
Fixed Amounts	Mortgage/Rent							
	Car Payments							
	Other Loans							
	Internet Access							
	Day Care							
	Insurance							
	Clubs/Dues							
	Savings							
	Allowance/Mad Money							
Fixed Variable	Electricity							
	Heating Oil/Gas							
	Water							
	Telephone/Cell Phone							
	Cable TV/Satellite/TiVo							
	Groceries							
	Meals Out							
	Auto Expense/Gas							
	Church/Charity							
Occasional	Household							
	Personal							
	Clothes/Dry Cleaning							
	Medical							
	Child Expense							
	Recreation							
Installment	Credit Cards:							
Total	Total Income							
	Total Expense							
	Total Excess							
	Total Short							

MONTHLY BUDGET WORKSHEET

INCOME SOURCE:							
Net Income Total Amount							

	Expenses	Amount	Date Due	Date Paid	Date Rcv.:			
Fixed Amounts	Mortgage/Rent							
	Car Payments							
	Other Loans							
	Internet Access							
	Day Care							
	Insurance							
	Clubs/Dues							
	Savings							
	Allowance/Mad Money							
Fixed Variable	Electricity							
	Heating Oil/Gas							
	Water							
	Telephone/Cell Phone							
	Cable TV/Satellite/TiVo							
	Groceries							
	Meals Out							
	Auto Expense/Gas							
	Church/Charity							
Occasional	Household							
	Personal							
	Clothes/Dry Cleaning							
	Medical							
	Child Expense							
	Recreation							
Installment	Credit Cards:							
Total	Total Income							
	Total Expense							
	Total Excess							
	Total Short							

MONTHLY BUDGET WORKSHEET

INCOME SOURCE:							
Net Income Total Amount							

	Expenses	Amount	Date Due	Date Paid	Date Rcv.:				
Fixed Amounts	Mortgage/Rent								
	Car Payments								
	Other Loans								
	Internet Access								
	Day Care								
	Insurance								
	Clubs/Dues								
	Savings								
	Allowance/Mad Money								
Fixed Variable	Electricity								
	Heating Oil/Gas								
	Water								
	Telephone/Cell Phone								
	Cable TV/Satellite/TiVo								
	Groceries								
	Meals Out								
	Auto Expense/Gas								
	Church/Charity								
Occasional	Household								
	Personal								
	Clothes / Dry Cleaning								
	Medical								
	Child Expense								
	Recreation								
Installment	Credit Cards:								
Total	**Total Income**								
	Total Expense								
	Total Excess								
	Total Short								

MONTHLY BUDGET WORKSHEET

APRIL

	INCOME SOURCE:			Date		Date				
	Net Income Total Amount									
	Expenses	**Amount**	**Due**	**Paid**	**Rcv.:**					
Fixed Amounts	Mortgage/Rent									
	Car Payments									
	Other Loans									
	Internet Access									
	Day Care									
	Insurance									
	Clubs/Dues									
	Savings									
	Allowance/Mad Money									
Fixed Variable	Electricity									
	Heating Oil/Gas									
	Water									
	Telephone/Cell Phone									
	Cable TV/Satellite/TiVo									
	Groceries									
	Meals Out									
	Auto Expense/Gas									
	Church/Charity									
Occasional	Household									
	Personal									
	Clothes/Dry Cleaning									
	Medical									
	Child Expense									
	Recreation									
Installment	Credit Cards:									
Total	**Total Income**									
	Total Expense									
	Total Excess									
	Total Short									

MONTHLY BUDGET WORKSHEET

INCOME SOURCE:							
Net Income Total Amount							

	Expenses	Amount	Date Due	Date Paid	Date Rcv.:			
Fixed Amounts	Mortgage/Rent							
	Car Payments							
	Other Loans							
	Internet Access							
	Day Care							
	Insurance							
	Clubs/Dues							
	Savings							
	Allowance/Mad Money							
Fixed Variable	Electricity							
	Heating Oil/Gas							
	Water							
	Telephone/Cell Phone							
	Cable TV/Satellite/TiVo							
	Groceries							
	Meals Out							
	Auto Expense/Gas							
	Church/Charity							
Occasional	Household							
	Personal							
	Clothes/Dry Cleaning							
	Medical							
	Child Expense							
	Recreation							
Installment	Credit Cards:							
Total	Total Income							
	Total Expense							
	Total Excess							
	Total Short							

MONTHLY BUDGET WORKSHEET

INCOME SOURCE:							
Net Income Total Amount							

	Expenses	Amount	Date Due	Date Paid	Date Rcv.:			
Fixed Amounts	Mortgage/Rent							
	Car Payments							
	Other Loans							
	Internet Access							
	Day Care							
	Insurance							
	Clubs/Dues							
	Savings							
	Allowance/Mad Money							
Fixed Variable	Electricity							
	Heating Oil/Gas							
	Water							
	Telephone/Cell Phone							
	Cable TV/Satellite/TiVo							
	Groceries							
	Meals Out							
	Auto Expense/Gas							
	Church/Charity							
Occasional	Household							
	Personal							
	Clothes/Dry Cleaning							
	Medical							
	Child Expense							
	Recreation							
Installment	Credit Cards:							
Total	**Total Income**							
	Total Expense							
	Total Excess							
	Total Short							

MONTHLY BUDGET WORKSHEET

INCOME SOURCE:								
Net Income Total Amount								

	Expenses	Amount	Date Due	Date Paid	Date Rcv.:			
Fixed Amounts	Mortgage/Rent							
	Car Payments							
	Other Loans							
	Internet Access							
	Day Care							
	Insurance							
	Clubs/Dues							
	Savings							
	Allowance/Mad Money							
Fixed Variable	Electricity							
	Heating Oil/Gas							
	Water							
	Telephone/Cell Phone							
	Cable TV/Satellite/TiVo							
	Groceries							
	Meals Out							
	Auto Expense/Gas							
	Church/Charity							
Occasional	Household							
	Personal							
	Clothes/Dry Cleaning							
	Medical							
	Child Expense							
	Recreation							
Installment	Credit Cards:							
Total	Total Income							
	Total Expense							
	Total Excess							
	Total Short							

MONTHLY BUDGET WORKSHEET

INCOME SOURCE:								
Net Income Total Amount								

	Expenses	Amount	Date Due	Date Paid	Date Rcv.:			
Fixed Amounts	Mortgage/Rent							
	Car Payments							
	Other Loans							
	Internet Access							
	Day Care							
	Insurance							
	Clubs/Dues							
	Savings							
	Allowance/Mad Money							
Fixed Variable	Electricity							
	Heating Oil/Gas							
	Water							
	Telephone/Cell Phone							
	Cable TV/Satellite/TiVo							
	Groceries							
	Meals Out							
	Auto Expense/Gas							
	Church/Charity							
Occasional	Household							
	Personal							
	Clothes/Dry Cleaning							
	Medical							
	Child Expense							
	Recreation							
Installment	Credit Cards:							
Total	Total Income							
	Total Expense							
	Total Excess							
	Total Short							

MONTHLY BUDGET WORKSHEET

SEPTEMBER

INCOME SOURCE:								
Net Income Total Amount								

Expenses	Amount	Date Due	Date Paid	Date Rcv.:				
Fixed Amounts								
Mortgage/Rent								
Car Payments								
Other Loans								
Internet Access								
Day Care								
Insurance								
Clubs/Dues								
Savings								
Allowance/Mad Money								
Fixed Variable								
Electricity								
Heating Oil/Gas								
Water								
Telephone/Cell Phone								
Cable TV/Satellite/TiVo								
Groceries								
Meals Out								
Auto Expense/Gas								
Church/Charity								
Occasional								
Household								
Personal								
Clothes/Dry Cleaning								
Medical								
Child Expense								
Recreation								
Installment								
Credit Cards:								
Total								
Total Income								
Total Expense								
Total Excess								
Total Short								

MONTHLY BUDGET WORKSHEET

INCOME SOURCE:								
Net Income Total Amount								

	Expenses	**Amount**	**Date**		**Date Rcv.:**				
			Due	**Paid**					
Fixed Amounts	Mortgage/Rent								
	Car Payments								
	Other Loans								
	Internet Access								
	Day Care								
	Insurance								
	Clubs/Dues								
	Savings								
	Allowance/Mad Money								
Fixed Variable	Electricity								
	Heating Oil/Gas								
	Water								
	Telephone/Cell Phone								
	Cable TV/Satellite/TiVo								
	Groceries								
	Meals Out								
	Auto Expense/Gas								
	Church/Charity								
Occasional	Household								
	Personal								
	Clothes/Dry Cleaning								
	Medical								
	Child Expense								
	Recreation								
Installment	Credit Cards:								
Total	**Total Income**								
	Total Expense								
	Total Excess								
	Total Short								

MONTHLY BUDGET WORKSHEET

NOVEMBER

INCOME SOURCE:								
Net Income Total Amount								

	Expenses	Amount	Date Due	Date Paid	Date Rcv.:			
Fixed Amounts	Mortgage/Rent							
	Car Payments							
	Other Loans							
	Internet Access							
	Day Care							
	Insurance							
	Clubs/Dues							
	Savings							
	Allowance/Mad Money							
Fixed Variable	Electricity							
	Heating Oil/Gas							
	Water							
	Telephone/Cell Phone							
	Cable TV/Satellite/TiVo							
	Groceries							
	Meals Out							
	Auto Expense/Gas							
	Church/Charity							
Occasional	Household							
	Personal							
	Clothes/Dry Cleaning							
	Medical							
	Child Expense							
	Recreation							
Installment	Credit Cards:							
Total	Total Income							
	Total Expense							
	Total Excess							
	Total Short							

MONTHLY BUDGET WORKSHEET

INCOME SOURCE:							
Net Income Total Amount							

	Expenses	Amount	Date Due	Date Paid	Date Rcv.:			
Fixed Amounts	Mortgage/Rent							
	Car Payments							
	Other Loans							
	Internet Access							
	Day Care							
	Insurance							
	Clubs/Dues							
	Savings							
	Allowance/Mad Money							
Fixed Variable	Electricity							
	Heating Oil/Gas							
	Water							
	Telephone/Cell Phone							
	Cable TV/Satellite/TiVo							
	Groceries							
	Meals Out							
	Auto Expense/Gas							
	Church/Charity							
Occasional	Household							
	Personal							
	Clothes/Dry Cleaning							
	Medical							
	Child Expense							
	Recreation							
Installment	Credit Cards:							
Total	**Total Income**							
	Total Expense							
	Total Excess							
	Total Short							

Variable Income Worksheet

"It took us about seven months, but now we finally have a handle on our erratic income. There were times when we would go three months without any kind of income. In the beginning, it seemed like all we were doing was dodging phone calls and juggling promises. But then, by carefully tracking and planning our expenses over time and working closely with the creditors, we were able to work out how much we needed every month to run the household. When we finally did get paid, we knew exactly what bills to pay, how much had to be covered, and what amount we needed to carry over into savings each time. What a difference this has made. We feel like we can breathe again!"

Planning your monthly finances can be especially challenging when your income is not predictable or regular each month. Often I hear people say they cannot create a budget because their income is based on commissions, self-employment, or other irregular income and therefore they feel they have no way to plan ahead. Actually, having a spending plan that gives you a clear outline of your basic monthly fixed expenses and a plan for covering them is even *more* important when your income is not regular.

I have met with many clients who have been in variable income situations, which is the reason I added this new worksheet. For many of those clients, utilizing all three of the main worksheets together—the **Yearly Budget Worksheet, Monthly Budget Worksheet**, and **Monthly Expense Record** (found in this section of the workbook)—worked most effectively. They were able to get a handle on the best approach for dealing with those three-month stretches of no income and then successfully plan the best way to distribute the bonus check or commission or other business income when it did come in.

This worksheet is designed to give you a guideline for planning a system that helps you know and cover your basic fixed monthly expenses every month, whether you receive income or not. *Without a clear long-range plan, it is very tempting to react to a large sum of money as a mini windfall. This worksheet will help you keep a big-picture perspective.* You will learn to plan proactively and stay prepared for upcoming financial obligations by saving the appropriate amount of money.

The key is starting with a conservative approach and stashing as much of the income as possible into savings *to act as your future monthly income.* This is especially true if you do not really know when the next amount of money will be coming in or how much. You may only know that it is very likely that the case will be settled, or the sale will close, or the partnership may have enough to pay salaries again, or the company will be giving some bonus distribution at some point. And yes, there is always the possibility that something can happen and the money may *not* come through.

That's why you want *contingency plans:* money in the bank; ability to cut back dramatically with the spending; good credit rating to help with access to loans; backup help from family or friends; other job possibilities; good relationships with all your creditors to work out short-term arrangements; attention to your investments to be sure they are performing well; and a reality check on the real cost of your cars and other personal property that you may want to sell or replace with less expensive versions.

As you work out the history or the current record of your irregular income, you may see that there actually is a pattern. With this pattern you can begin to coordinate some of your big-ticket payments, such as annual or semiannual insurances, tuition, or taxes, with the timing of the income. Clients have often been amazed to realize how much power they had over their finances once they were armed with information. Many times you can make arrangements for totally different payment dates and even payments if you have a clear outlined plan and you discuss it with a receptive customer service representative or supervisor for that company.

There may be many months when no money is coming in and you are living solely on the savings you have set aside specifically for those months. *Continue to stay conscious of your spending and money patterns during this time. Even though living that way can be unsettling, remember to pat yourself on the back for having the foresight and prudence to put sufficient funds aside.*

How to Use this Worksheet

The purpose of the **Variable Income Worksheet** is twofold. First, it serves as a planner for projecting upcoming income to the best of your ability. Second, once the actual income comes in and you record this information, you will have a record to refer to next year when projecting the new year. I usually suggest you use pencil or have a way to easily change your numbers because this whole book is a *workbook* and your work is always in progress.

Windfall Planner

Before starting on this **Variable Income Worksheet**, it may help to review the **Windfall Planner** worksheet on page 94. The **Windfall Planner** is helpful for those one-time lump sums of money, such as an insurance settlement, inheritance, or company bonus. Using that planner helps you to see the many options to consider and to then prioritize the distribution of those funds.

Multiple Sales Monthly Planner

If you are in sales, before you begin this **Variable Income Worksheet**, I want you to know about the **Multiple Sales Monthly Planner** on pages 96–98. As you know, variable commission income could be from multiple closings on products and projects as well as from one big commission check. To help itemize all those different possible closing amounts, I have added an accessory planner. With this planner, you will have a way to record those sales that are projected, listed, pending, or sold for each month. Once you have completed the total amount of actual closings, you can transfer that monthly total to the **Variable Income Worksheet** under "Income Source."

Variable Income

Income Source

A variety of income sources are listed on pages 89–90. If your source does not fit any of these categories, cross them out and insert your own. When you know the amount or approximate amount of the bonus, commission trust or investment distribution, or other income source, enter that amount in the column under the appropriate month.

If you know the month but have no clue what the figure will be, such as with dividends or royalties, place an "X" in the box under the month to remind you when some money should be arriving. This also acts as a reminder in the event some expected money has not arrived, and you can then follow up on the delay.

Once that large check does arrive, the critical step is to evaluate how best to distribute those funds. What do you pay off first? How much do you save? How much do you need to live on for this month and possibly many more months? The following sections will help you determine the best ways to use the money, including *how much money you will need, how much to put aside in savings, and how much debt you can pay off.*

Basic Monthly Household and Personal Expenses

Estimated Taxes/Savings

After you finish relishing the nice bonus package royalty or commission check that just came in, remember that the very next step is addressing the taxes. If taxes have not been withdrawn from this particular source of income, then this is the place to start and make sure you calculate how much to put aside for taxes. Enter this amount on page 91 on the top row.

There are enough resources to advise you where the best place is for "parking" your money while saving it. You may already work with a tax accountant or financial planner who can advise you on where and how much to save. As a general guideline, I recommend putting aside approximately 25 to 30 percent as a minimum starting place for your basic commissions and other job income. The most important point is to do it. Move that money over to savings, a money market account, CD, or whatever seems most appropriate right away so you are dealing with realistic numbers as you plan your budget. Some people find it easier to dedicate a separate savings account for taxes only so they are not tempted to use that money for other household expenses or emergencies.

The goal throughout this workbook is to help you to manage your finances proactively instead of reactively. Ignoring the tax issue or saying you will take more money out of the next check for taxes because this time you really need all the money, starts to set you up for that reactive crisis management cycle once again. This time you can change that cycle. Be patient and know you *can* turn things around. Outline this plan and follow it as closely as you can.

Note about Stock Options

In the world of stock options, severance payouts, and other money packages, it is more important than ever to pay attention to the tax consequences. It is not unusual to see more than 50 percent in the end going to taxes depending on your income bracket and other factors. I have witnessed a lot of financial havoc for clients who had not withdrawn enough for taxes. Large sums of money can easily draw you in emotionally and skew your good judgement. Be sure to talk with a tax accountant for an accurate projection before buying that new patio set or car with cash.

Fixed and Variable Expenses

The next step on page 91 is the **Basic Monthly Household and Personal Expenses** worksheet. I recommend completing the **Monthly Budget Worksheet** starting on page 69 and the **Monthly Expense Record** starting on page 126 to help you use this section more efficiently. The design does allow planning from this form exclusively; however, the other worksheets are more comprehensive so there is less chance of overlooking any critical expenses.

If you have been using the **Monthly Expense Record** for *tracking* your daily spending and have good records of all your fixed bills and general expenses, then those totals can easily be transferred to this worksheet. The **Monthly Budget Worksheet** allows more room for *projecting* your monthly plan of any upcoming bills and other unique expenses for the month.

Just a reminder, the **Monthly Budget Worksheet** is the beginning step if you don't have a history of expenses yet. This worksheet offers you a guideline to think about and project the many areas beyond the bills where money may be spent during each month.

Credit Cards

Once the basic living expenses are handled, it is time to calculate how much to pay toward the credit card balances. In an ideal world, the only credit card balances would be those that are paid off each month. Until that time arrives, use this worksheet to pay off your credit card balances as quickly as possible and not waste another dime on finance charges, late fees, and over-the-limit fees. The **Debt Payoff Record** (starting on page 101) can help you ultimately get on top of the debt situation.

If planning to make payments on the credit card debt is particularly difficult one month because of the low income and high fixed expenses, still try to find some way to pay the minimum due plus an extra ten dollars on each of the credit cards. This small additional amount will save you substantially over the long run.

During those months when a large sum of money is received, take this opportunity to pay down or off some or all of your credit card debt. Of course, a lot depends on the overall plan, your future income, and your future needs. *Find a balance in this plan so you pay off enough of the credit card bill to save you significant finance charges and yet have enough funds to be prepared for future months of no income.*

Major Periodic Expenses

The missing link in most budgets is the lack of planning for periodic expenses that show up throughout the year as quarterly, annual, or periodic expenses but are not part of the monthly picture.

The **Yearly Budget Worksheet** on page 53 will help you determine what periodic expenses exist and which ones are imperative to pay. If you have not yet completed this section, go ahead and review pages 51–52 for a suggested list of expenses that may apply to your situation right now. Transfer these totals to the worksheet on pages 89–90 under the appropriate monthly column.

Deposit to or Withdraw from Savings

Add your total income and total expenses under each month on this form. The idea here is to see how much money is left over or is short after taking care of all the basic needs outlined above. Once you can see that total amount in black and white, you can again take some constructive action. Depositing money into savings can be extremely satisfying after having a long stretch of debt and very little income.

For those surplus months, be sure to stash that excess money right away. If you have completed all the information for all months, it will be very apparent which months you will be needing to withdraw from savings to cover the expenses. The **Windfall Planner** on page 94 is another tool available for you in the event you unexpectedly receive a large sum of money.

There may still be situations where you can't predict when the next month will be a surplus or even an income month for you. In those cases, maximum savings is critical along with clear contingency plans as mentioned earlier. *At some point, if this unpredictable income continues too long and erodes your savings, lifestyle, and personal well-being, you may want to reevaluate your work options or even where you now live.*

Remember, when you have knowledge, you have more power to make decisions. Use this section as your road map to a more powerful financial future.

"We continue to use these tools beyond our coaching time with Judy because of their value to our planning. Since I'm self-employed and my husband has a part-time business, our income fluctuates every month. These tools help us set goals and give us the freedom to plan for things we want, not only our obligations."

—Joan F., CA

VARIABLE INCOME WORKSHEET

Income Source	Jan.	Feb.	Mar.	Apr.	May	June
Investment Income _____ _____						
Commissions _____ _____						
Bonus _____ _____						
Business Income _____ _____						
Consultant _____ _____						
Reimbursement _____ _____						
Freelance _____ _____						
Royalty _____ _____						
Other* _____ _____ _____						
TOTAL INCOME						

*Tax refund, cash gifts, inheritance, trust, gratuities, rental property, insurance settlement, property sale, affiliate website sales, etc.

VARIABLE INCOME WORKSHEET

Income Source	July	Aug.	Sept.	Oct.	Nov.	Dec.	Total
Investment Income							
Commissions							
Bonus							
Business Income							
Consultant							
Reimbursement							
Freelance							
Royalty							
Other*							
TOTAL INCOME							

*Tax refund, cash gifts, inheritance, trust, gratuities, rental property, insurance settlement, property sale, affiliate website sales, etc.

BASIC MONTHLY HOUSEHOLD AND PERSONAL EXPENSES

(Refer to Monthly Budget Worksheet and Yearly Budget Worksheet for more comprehensive categories.)

Expense	Jan.	Feb.	Mar.	Apr.	May	June
Estimated Taxes						
Fixed: Mortgage/Rent						
Car Payment/Lease						
_____						
Loans						
_____						
Insurance						
_____						
_____						
Variable: Utilities						
Phones						
Groceries						
Gasoline						
_____						
_____						
Credit Cards:						
_____						
_____						
_____						
Major Periodic Expenses (p. 54)						
TOTAL EXPENSES						
Total Income (pp. 89–90)						
Difference						
Deposit into Savings*						
Withdraw from Savings						

*If extra funds are available this month, see the Windfall Planner on page 94.

BASIC MONTHLY HOUSEHOLD AND PERSONAL EXPENSES

(Refer to Monthly Budget Worksheet and Yearly Budget Worksheet for more comprehensive categories.)

Expense	July	Aug.	Sept.	Oct.	Nov.	Dec.
Estimated Taxes						
Fixed: Mortgage/Rent						
Car Payment/Lease						
Loans						
Insurance						
Variable: Utilities						
Phones						
Groceries						
Gasoline						
Credit Cards:						
Major Periodic Expenses (p. 54)						
TOTAL EXPENSES						
Total Income (pp. 89–90)						
Difference						
Deposit into Savings*						
Withdraw from Savings						

*If extra funds are available this month, see the Windfall Planner on page 94.

Windfall Planner

Use this planner to outline a reasonable plan for prioritizing the distribution of lump sums of money, such as tax refunds, an inheritance, insurance settlements, company bonuses, severance packages, sale of a home, cash gifts, royalties, auction or yard sales, and any other sources.

Be sure to have the expected or promised money actually in hand (in your bank) before making any payments or purchases. And don't forget to handle any taxes that will be due up front if they have not yet been taken out.

For peace of mind and balance, consider paying portions to the *past, present,* and *future.* Pay off past debts, buy something on your wish list, and set aside money for future needs.

WINDFALL PLANNER

Date: _____

Source of Money: _____

Total Amount: _____

Possible Expense Item	Amount	or	Percent
Estimated Taxes to Put in Savings (if no taxes have been taken out)	$ _____		_____ %
Catch Up on Payments Currently Behind	_____		_____
Back Taxes Still Due (federal, state, property)	_____		_____
Credit Card(s)—Pay Down or Off	_____		_____
Credit Card(s)—Pay Down or Off	_____		_____
Loan(s)—Pay Down or Off	_____		_____
Loan(s)—Pay Down or Off	_____		_____
Cover _____ No. of Months of Living Expenses (Put this in savings.)	_____		_____
Stock Up on Household and/or Grocery Items	_____		_____
Upcoming Major Expense(s) (See Yearly Budget Worksheet on p. 54.)	_____		_____
Reserve Savings Account (See Yearly Budget Worksheet on p. 54.)	_____		_____
Emergency Savings Account	_____		_____
Home Improvement Project(s)	_____		_____
New Purchases	_____		_____
Investments/Retirement/College	_____		_____
Vacation/Travel/Trips/Fun Money	_____		_____
Charitable Giving	_____		_____
Other _____	_____		_____
_____	_____		_____
_____	_____		_____
_____	_____		_____
_____	_____		_____
_____	_____		_____
_____	_____		_____
_____	_____		_____
_____	_____		_____
_____	_____		_____
_____	_____		_____
_____	_____		_____
GRAND TOTAL	$ _____		_____ %

Multiple Sales Monthly Planner

Whether you are an interior decorator in a home furnishing store, a REALTOR®, or a software salesperson, if your income is based on commission, this **Multiple Sales Monthly Planner** is designed to help you get a handle on those ongoing monthly sales activities.

The goal is to have one place to list all your projected, pending, and closing sales for each month and to keep the form open enough to allow for the many changes that occur throughout the month. This is another place it would be wise to use pencil.

Use this planner as an addendum to the forms you already use through your work. It can also be used to determine your variable income for each month, which you can record on the various worksheets in this workbook. This form is deliberately kept generic to address the unique needs of different sales environments.

You may need to alter code titles listed on the bottom of the planner, depending on the line of work you are in and, in some cases, they may not apply at all. The date as well as the amount for closing a sale or making a potential sale could be known or approximate; again, put down the information that works best for your needs.

Modify this planner as much as you need so it is a functional tool for you.

MULTIPLE SALES MONTHLY PLANNER

JANUARY

Code	Sales (Customer/Product)	Date	Amount

Notes:

Total Income $ _____

FEBRUARY

Code	Sales (Customer/Product)	Date	Amount

Notes:

Total Income $ _____

MARCH

Code	Sales (Customer/Product)	Date	Amount

Notes:

Total Income $ _____

APRIL

Code	Sales (Customer/Product)	Date	Amount

Notes:

Total Income $ _____

Code: F—Future Prospect/Project   L—Listing of a Sale   P—Pending Sale   S—Sold and Closed

MULTIPLE SALES MONTHLY PLANNER

MAY

Code	Sales (Customer/Product)	Date	Amount

Notes:

Total Income $ _____

JUNE

Code	Sales (Customer/Product)	Date	Amount

Notes:

Total Income $ _____

JULY

Code	Sales (Customer/Product)	Date	Amount

Notes:

Total Income $ _____

AUGUST

Code	Sales (Customer/Product)	Date	Amount

Notes:

Total Income $ _____

Code: F—Future Prospect/Project   L—Listing of a Sale   P—Pending Sale   S—Sold and Closed

MULTIPLE SALES MONTHLY PLANNER

Code	Sales (Customer/Product)	Date	Amount

Notes:

Total Income $ _____

OCTOBER

Code	Sales (Customer/Product)	Date	Amount

Notes:

Total Income $ _____

NOVEMBER

Code	Sales (Customer/Product)	Date	Amount

Notes:

Total Income $ _____

DECEMBER

Code	Sales (Customer/Product)	Date	Amount

Notes:

Total Income $ _____

Code: F—Future Prospect/Project   L—Listing of a Sale   P—Pending Sale   S—Sold and Closed

Debt Payoff Record

*"In two years' time, we went from $16,000 debt to $2,000 (vehicles)
and saved over $10,000. It took facing the numbers in the workbook,
seeing what we spent every day, realizing how much money was
going to finance charges, and getting out of our denial about debt.
Now we still buy clothes and go on vacations. The difference is the
planning and saving ahead of time."*

When to Use this Worksheet

If you are beginning to get deep in debt or just need a better idea of how much
you still owe on all your bills, such as medical expenses, car loan, finance
company loan, credit cards, or department store cards, this **Debt Payoff
Record** worksheet starting on page 101 is an important step for regaining
financial control.

Staying organized is easier as well, as you now have a way to keep all
your credit information in one simple place. You can also list the creditor's
address and contact name, if you need this information frequently, in the
blank space at the top or bottom of the page.

What to Include

The expenses to include are those you are unable to pay in full and which
must extend over a period of time (installment payments), such as auto-
mobile, home equity, student, or finance company loans; medical, legal,
or family loans; IRS debt; and all credit card charges. This worksheet will
clearly show you how much you have paid, what you still owe, and how
much it is costing you to pay in installments. *Remember, every penny you pay
for finance charges is money you could have in your pocket for savings or vacations
if the bills were paid in full.*

How to Start

Start by filling in all the information at the top of the worksheet, such as the
creditor's name and account number, for each debt you have. The "Total

Balance Due" at the top gives you your starting figure so you can watch your progress. It will also be helpful to add the date somewhere on the top of this worksheet so you know your total beginning balance as of a specific date if you are not starting this form in January. Be sure to include the annual percentage rate (APR), which lets you know what interest rate you are paying.

As you make payments each month, take time to actually look at your whole statement. I know the tendency is to zero in on the "Minimum Payment Due" block and ignore the rest. It's time to start paying attention to the other information on the statement like "New Balance," "Finance Charge," "Late Payment Fee," and "Over the Limit Fee." Granted, it's very difficult to acknowledge the whole picture, yet this is an important step and it's how you will begin to take charge and change your spending habits.

Fill in the "Amount Paid" and "Balance Due" for each month on this worksheet. The "Interest/Penalty" line is for all the finance charges and other fees. Just adding up that line across both pages will certainly get your attention each month.

Now really look at that statement and notice how much of the minimum payment you pay is for the finance charge and how much is actually payment toward the balance due. Amazing, isn't it? Now you see why it is taking so long to get out of debt.

"I absolutely HAVE to tell you what a difference your book The Budget Kit *has made for me. I'm a 31-year-old single female who got into trouble with credit cards. I have lived in Davenport, IA, for a little over two years and had never been free of credit card debt the entire time, until just a few months ago. I used every excuse to spend money. It's been a hard week at work, I need to get out of the house, I deserve a little treat, I haven't bought myself anything for a while, or to decorate at home. I finally got to a point where I hated to get the mail. It was always bills and stressed me out! I went through every emotion you can imagine, from anger that I had let my credit card debt get so high, to embarrassment that this was the second time in my life I'd had financial issues, to feeling hopeless about getting my financial life together again. I was depressed and would cry and just feel so fed up with the whole thing. I knew something had to change.*

It is a truly amazing thing what discipline and direction will do for a person! I have all my credit cards paid off—and put away."

—Kerri H., IA

DEBT PAYOFF RECORD

CREDITOR						Total*
			Loans			
Account Number						
Total Balance Due						
Phone Number						
Interest Rate (APR)						
January						
Amount Paid						
Interest/Penalty						
Balance Due						
February						
Amount Paid						
Interest/Penalty						
Balance Due						
March						
Amount Paid						
Interest/Penalty						
Balance Due						
April						
Amount Paid						
Interest/Penalty						
Balance Due						
May						
Amount Paid						
Interest/Penalty						
Balance Due						
June						
Amount Paid						
Interest/Penalty						
Balance Due						
July						
Amount Paid						
Interest/Penalty						
Balance Due						
August						
Amount Paid						
Interest/Penalty						
Balance Due						
September						
Amount Paid						
Interest/Penalty						
Balance Due						
October						
Amount Paid						
Interest/Penalty						
Balance Due						
November						
Amount Paid						
Interest/Penalty						
Balance Due						
December						
Amount Paid						
Interest/Penalty						
Balance Due						
Balance Due						

*Add your total for loan debt to the Grand Total column on page 103.

DEBT PAYOFF RECORD

CREDITOR	Credit Cards					Total*
Account Number						
Total Balance Due						
Phone Number						
Interest Rate (APR)						
January						
Amount Paid						
Interest/Penalty						
Balance Due						
February						
Amount Paid						
Interest/Penalty						
Balance Due						
March						
Amount Paid						
Interest/Penalty						
Balance Due						
April						
Amount Paid						
Interest/Penalty						
Balance Due						
May						
Amount Paid						
Interest/Penalty						
Balance Due						
June						
Amount Paid						
Interest/Penalty						
Balance Due						
July						
Amount Paid						
Interest/Penalty						
Balance Due						
August						
Amount Paid						
Interest/Penalty						
Balance Due						
September						
Amount Paid						
Interest/Penalty						
Balance Due						
October						
Amount Paid						
Interest/Penalty						
Balance Due						
November						
Amount Paid						
Interest/Penalty						
Balance Due						
December						
Amount Paid						
Interest/Penalty						
Balance Due						
Balance Due						

*Add your total for credit card debt to the Grand Total column on page 103.

DEBT PAYOFF RECORD

CREDITOR	Other (Medical, Legal, Personal, etc.)				Total	Grand Total
Account Number						
Total Balance Due						
Phone Number						
Interest Rate (APR)						
January						
Amount Paid						
Interest/Penalty						
Balance Due						
February						
Amount Paid						
Interest/Penalty						
Balance Due						
March						
Amount Paid						
Interest/Penalty						
Balance Due						
April						
Amount Paid						
Interest/Penalty						
Balance Due						
May						
Amount Paid						
Interest/Penalty						
Balance Due						
June						
Amount Paid						
Interest/Penalty						
Balance Due						
July						
Amount Paid						
Interest/Penalty						
Balance Due						
August						
Amount Paid						
Interest/Penalty						
Balance Due						
September						
Amount Paid						
Interest/Penalty						
Balance Due						
October						
Amount Paid						
Interest/Penalty						
Balance Due						
November						
Amount Paid						
Interest/Penalty						
Balance Due						
December						
Amount Paid						
Interest/Penalty						
Balance Due						
Balance Due						

Cost of Credit Card Purchases

Have you ever wondered how long it would take to pay off your credit card debt? Chart A below shows an example of what you would pay if you only paid the minimum payment on a $2,000 balance and then what you would pay with just an extra 25 cents a day, or about $7.50 a month.

When comparing the different minimum *percent* payments on Chart A, the smaller minimum percent (2 percent) certainly looks more appealing when looking at the resulting lower minimum payment ($40) for Card A. Now notice

CHART A: THE COST OF CREDIT CARD PURCHASES
BALANCE $2,000

	TOTAL COST WHEN PAYING ONLY THE MINIMUM PAYMENT					SAVINGS WHEN ADDING AN EXTRA $.25/DAY TO PAYMENT		
CARD	Interest Rate	Minimum Percent Payment	Minimum Payment	Total Interest Cost	Years* to Pay-off	Interest Paid after Extra $.25/Day	Total Interest Saved	Years* Saved by Extra $.25/Day
CARD A	19.8 %	2 %	$40	$7,636	42	$2,720	$4,916	28
CARD B	19.8	2.78	56	2,585	17	1,557	1,029	8
CARD C	12.5	2	40	1,840	18	1,071	769	8
CARD D	8.25	3	60	542	10	400	142	3

*This information was in months, which was rounded up to make the extra year.

Source: These figures were calculated by Marc Eisenson of *www.goodadvicepress.com,* author of *The Banker's Secret* and coauthor of *Reduce Debt, Reduce Stress: Real Life Solutions for Solving Your Credit Crisis* (Good Advice Press, 2009) and *Invest in Yourself: Six Secrets to a Rich Life* (Wiley, 2001).

CHART B: WHAT A DIFFERENCE A FRACTION OF A PERCENT MAKES
Based on $5,000 Credit Card Balance and 17% Interest Rate

Credit Cards	Card Minimum % Payment	First Month's Payment	Total Interest Paid	Years to Pay Off
Card A	1.67%	$83.50	$25,354	81
Card B	2.00%	$100.00	$11,304	40
Card C	2.50%	$125.00	$6,210	24
Card D	3.00%	$150.00	$4,296	18

Total amount that will be paid: add to the $5,000 original balance.

Isn't it amazing that the same credit card debt of $5,000, at the same interest rate, can cost you anywhere between $4,296 and $25,354 in interest?

Source: This table is reprinted with permission from *Reduce Debt, Reduce Stress: Real Life Solutions for Solving Your Credit Crisis,* table 5, page 150, (Good Advice Press, 2009), by Gerri Detweiler, Nancy Castleman, and Marc Eisenson. *www.reducedebtreducestress.com*

how much it adds to the "Total Interest Cost" ($7,636) and the number of "Years to Pay-Off" needed (42 years) to eliminate the debt. You can see why it really does take "forever" to pay off your debt!

The remainder of Chart A on the right shows the savings by just adding 25 cents a day to your minimum payment or $7.50 a month. For that same example mentioned above, you would save $4,916 in interest, not to mention the 28 years of payments that would be eliminated.

Now let's see what a difference making a $125 monthly (2.5 percent) minimum payment versus a $100 (2 percent) minimum payment would be with a $5,000 credit card balance and a 17 percent interest rate. Look on Chart B on page 104 under the interest column. You would save $5,094 and 16 years. What a savings an extra $25 a month can make!

Have I gotten your attention yet? The whole point is to increase those credit card payments above the minimum as much as you can. If you can pay the extra $100 or more each month, as many try to do, then go for it. If not, know that every effort you can make to pay some extra amount can have huge dividends for you in the long run.

> *"I have also been using the Debt Payoff Worksheet to help track my process in eliminating my debt and plan to eliminate one credit card debt, car loan, and student loan (totaling $13,000) by August next year. I have my plan written down and check my progress monthly. I also strapped down on my spending (my daughter really dislikes this).* **By not paying attention to the whole picture, I had no idea what type of hole I was digging for myself.** *Thanks for everything."*
>
> —Leslie C., CA

One more note regarding minimum payments. With new federal guidelines, it may no longer be possible to make the bare minimum 2 percent of balance payments as shown in Chart A and carry the balance "forever." Credit card companies have started doubling their minimum payments. On a new card, the minimum payment is probably now closer to 4 percent of the total balance due. Also, for those of you who have been diligently making your monthly payments, don't be fooled by the tempting occasional "zero minimum payment due" on your statement. Continue to make a minimum payment every month and start using at least 4 percent of the current balance due as a base amount to pay. Like everything else related to credit cards, be sure to monitor your cards and all the insert notices carefully. These companies can and often do change the rules anytime, including the annual percentage rate (APR) and minimum payment due.

Becoming Debt-Free

Charts C and D are designed to encourage you and show you it is possible to be debt-free. In Chart C on page 106, an arbitrary 14 percent average is used for total debt, which could be a consolidation loan. My goal is to give you a sense of possibility. Find your total debt due in the left-hand column and then pick the amount you can afford each month, or the number of years you want to set as your goal to be debt-free, in the columns to the right. Once you know that figure, you can start to do whatever it takes to make that monthly payment happen and get your debt paid off.

Let's say your goal is to be debt-free in three or five years. Use Chart D on page 107 to find your interest rate and then pick your payments according to the three- or five-year plans and total debt due.

There are many books, software packages, and websites available to help you learn how to reduce your debt. These charts are provided merely as a sample to *motivate you to find the resources you need.*

The information in these charts is from the authors of *Reduce Debt, Reduce Stress: Real Life Solutions for Solving Your Credit Crisis.* Gerri Detweiler, Marc Eisenson, and Nancy Castleman have done a fantastic job of bringing together some of the most comprehensive, easy-to-read, and practical tips, examples, resources, and strategies I have seen. They provide nearly a dozen tables showing you how to reduce your credit card and mortgage debt (see *www.goodadvicepress.com*).

CHART C: HOW SOON CAN YOU BE DEBT-FREE?

The following figures are based on a debt with an average 14 percent interest rate.

If you want your debt paid off in the following years, see the chart below to find out how much your monthly payment would be to reach your debt-free goal.

Total Debt Due	1 Yr.	2 Yrs.	3 Yrs.	4 Yrs.	5 Yrs.	6 Yrs.	7 Yrs.	8 Yrs.	9 Yrs.	10 Yrs.
$ 3,000	$ 270	$ 144	$ 103	$ 82	$ 70	$ 62	$ 56	$ 52	$ 49	$ 47
5,000	449	240	171	137	116	103	94	87	82	78
10,000	898	480	342	273	233	206	187	174	163	155
15,000	1,347	720	513	410	349	309	281	261	245	233
20,000	1,796	960	684	547	465	412	375	347	327	311
25,000	2,245	1,200	854	683	582	515	469	434	408	388
30,000	2,694	1,440	1,025	820	698	618	562	521	490	466
35,000	3,143	1,680	1,196	956	814	721	656	608	572	543
40,000	3,591	1,921	1,367	1,093	931	824	750	695	653	621
45,000	4,040	2,161	1,538	1,230	1,047	927	843	782	735	699
50,000	4,489	2,401	1,709	1,366	1,163	1,030	937	869	817	776
75,000	6,734	3,601	2,563	2,049	1,745	1,545	1,406	1,303	1,225	1,165

Total Monthly Payment

Source: These figures were calculated by Marc Eisenson of *www.goodadvicepress.com*, author of *The Banker's Secret* and coauthor of *Reduce Debt, Reduce Stress: Real Life Solutions for Solving Your Credit Crisis* (Good Advice Press, 2009) and *Invest in Yourself: Six Secrets to a Rich Life* (Wiley, 2001).

Total Debt Due	Years	Consolidation Loan Rate						
		8%	9%	10%	11%	12%	13%	14%
$ 5,000	3	$ 157	$ 159	$ 161	$ 164	$ 166	$ 168	$ 171
	5	101	104	106	109	111	114	116
7,500	3	235	239	242	246	249	253	256
	5	152	156	159	163	167	171	175
10,000	3	313	318	323	327	332	337	342
	5	203	208	212	217	222	228	233
12,500	3	392	398	403	409	415	421	427
	5	253	259	266	272	278	284	291
15,000	3	470	477	484	491	498	505	513
	5	304	311	319	326	334	341	349
17,500	3	548	557	565	573	581	590	598
	5	355	363	372	381	389	398	407
20,000	3	627	636	645	655	664	674	684
	5	406	415	425	435	445	455	465
25,000	3	783	795	807	818	830	842	854
	5	507	519	531	544	556	569	582
30,000	3	940	954	968	982	996	1,011	1,025
	5	608	623	637	652	667	683	698
35,000	3	1,097	1,113	1,129	1,146	1,163	1,179	1,196
	5	710	727	744	761	779	796	814
40,000	3	1,253	1,272	1,291	1,310	1,329	1,348	1,367
	5	811	830	850	870	890	910	931
45,000	3	1,410	1,431	1,452	1,473	1,495	1,516	1,538
	5	912	934	956	978	1,001	1,024	1,047
50,000	3	1,567	1,590	1,613	1,637	1,661	1,685	1,709
	5	1,014	1,038	1,062	1,087	1,112	1,138	1,163

CHART D: PICK A MONTHLY PAYMENT TO PAY YOUR DEBT OFF IN THREE TO FIVE YEARS

Source: This table is reprinted with permission from *Reduce Debt, Reduce Stress: Real Life Solutions for Solving Your Credit Crisis* (Good Advice Press, 2009), by Gerri Detweiler, Nancy Castleman, and Marc Eisenson. *www. reducedebtreducestress.com*

Steps for Getting Out of Debt

After you pay off one debt, apply that same payment amount to another debt, preferably one with the highest interest, to shorten the term of that debt. An exception is if you have a smaller debt (even those with a lower interest rate) and you need the psychological satisfaction of making progress, then pay off that debt as soon as you can. As you continue to apply payments from paid-off debt to remaining debt, you will start to see how soon and how much of your total debt will be paid off in a few years.

By the following year, through the conscientious use of the worksheets in this workbook, you may no longer need this worksheet. Hurrah! As one reader put it, "This Debt Payoff Record form makes the whole workbook worth hugging a thousand times!"

Want Your Credit Card Paid Off in 11 Months?

With the following three factors in place, you can pay off any credit card balance in 11 months:

1. The interest rate is **less than 20 percent.**
2. You pay **10 percent** of the current **balance** and make that **same payment** every single month.
3. There is **no additional charging** on your credit card.

For example, if your balance is $5,000, you would pay $500 every single month. If your balance was $7,500, you would pay $750 every month. The total amount of finance charge you are paying overall will vary depending on the interest rate, but the 11 months to pay off the total balance will stay the same provided your interest rate is under 20 percent.

	Monthly Payment Needed to Be Debt-Free in 11 Months				
Credit Card	**Total Debt**	**× 10%**	**=**	**Monthly Payment**	
Mastercard	$ 5,000	× 10%	=	$ 500	
_____	$_____	× 10%	=	$_____	
_____	$_____	× 10%	=	$_____	
_____	$_____	× 10%	=	$_____	

This is a *rough estimate* of how long it will take you to pay off each card. Remember, the higher the interest rate and the lower the payment, the more months it will normally take to pay off. *The key is the constant monthly payment of the same amount regardless of the changing balance due.*

Remember, these are *very general* guidelines to give you a quick snapshot of an estimate. For much more accurate information which will factor in the compounding aspect of interest rates, use a business calculator. If you have online access, the simplest solution is to go to any of the following online calculators or your own favorite calculator websites and plug in your balance due, interest rate, and monthly payments or percent of balance you want to pay:

Online Financial Calculators:
- *http://cgi.money.cnn.com/tools/debtplanner/debtplanner.jsp*
- *www.bankrate.com/brm/calc/creditcardpay.asp*
- *http://calculators.aol.com/tools/aol/card04/tool.fcs*

- *www.cardratings.com/calculatorframe.html*
- *www.cardtrak.com/calculators/PayoffCC.html*
- *http://choosetosave.org/calculators*
- *www.credit.com/calculators/cc_debt*
- *www.dollartimes.com*
- *www.kiplinger.com/tools*
- *www.mindyourfinances.com/calculators/credit-card-payoff*
- *www.walletpop.com/calculators/credit-debt*

How Long Will It Take to Pay Off Your 0 Percent Rate Credit Card?

If you are looking for a quick snapshot of the length of time needed to pay off your credit cards based on how much you can pay each month and have a 0 percent interest rate the whole time, you can do the following exercise.

Credit Card	Total Debt	÷	Monthly Payment	=	Months to Pay Off	
Visa	$ 5,000	÷	$ 150	=	33 months	(2 yrs and 9 months)
___	$___	÷	$___	=	___ months	
___	$___	÷	$___	=	___ months	
___	$___	÷	$___	=	___ months	

Getting Control of Your Finances

When you reach the point where you become a wise and responsible consumer and you use credit to your advantage only as a means of using someone else's money and paying the bill in full when it is due, you will know you truly have control of your finances! You will also have much greater financial peace of mind.

Making Money Instead of Spending Money

"Those who understand interest collect it, and those who don't pay it."

—William H. Stone

Once you have gotten into the habit of making payments and applying extra money from paid-off debt to reducing the remaining debt, you will have acquired a great skill. When your debts are paid off, you can continue the payment schedule, only this time putting money into your savings and investments. *All that money that was used to pay off the debt-plus-interest and penalty charges now can go toward your savings. Instead of spending money, you will actually be making money on the same payment amounts.*

Let's see what kind of money you could be making. Chart E gives you an idea of just how much money. Using the same $2,000 credit card balance example from Chart A, look what can happen if you *invested* $2,000 at 10 percent instead of *spending* $2,000 at 19.8 percent. Rather than paying off the $2,000 debt for 42 years and *paying* $7,636 in interest, you would be *earning* $131,072 (compounded monthly) in 40 years. Not bad for only a $2,000 investment. Granted, 10 or 14 percent may be pretty tough to find these days. The point is that *any* percent will show you significant earnings over time.

CHART E: $2,000 ONE-TIME INVESTMENT— NO ANNUAL CONTRIBUTIONS

Years	6%	10%	14%
10	$ 3,639	$ 5,414	$ 8,045
20	6,620	14,656	32,361
30	12,045	39,675	130,169
40	24,702	131,072	691,672

Calculations were compounded monthly.

Source: These figures were calculated by Marc Eisenson of *www.goodadvicepress. com*, author of *The Banker's Secret* and coauthor of *Reduce Debt, Reduce Stress: Real Life Solutions for Solving Your Credit Crisis* (Good Advice Press, 2009) and *Invest in Yourself: Six Secrets to a Rich Life* (Wiley, 2001).

Fortunately, there are now numerous website resources and calculators for finding and evaluating investments and higher returns. By researching and finding higher investment returns, you can see the payoff for investing over 10 to 40 years.

Don't let the recent Great Recession discourage you from investing. Use that experience, and all insights and discernment you gained, to do your own initial due diligence and proper research. Not only is it important to research the different investments but also the financial adviser you choose to work with as well. Once you are armed with appropriate information, choose the investment route that best fits your financial, emotional, and risk-tolerance style. Don't forget to take advantage of any matching investment programs offered by your employer. Your goal is to find assets that keep your money working for you.

Best of all, when you start investing, not only will you have assets instead of debts, you will feel motivated, encouraged, excited, and confident about your financial skills.

"Thank you for getting us jump-started! It was most helpful to see which debts to focus on so we could prioritize our debt-payoff plan. We buckled down to really change and pay attention to our spending, and now we are so inspired to pay off our final debts that we have hired a financial planner to help us invest our newfound money."

GETTING ONLINE HELP FOR DEBT

As of this printing, there are numerous Internet-based nonprofit organizations and for-profit companies and practitioners providing financial information, services, counseling (in person, by phone, or on the Internet), coaching, and support.

Unfortunately, over the years many unscrupulous debt management firms have cropped up that take advantage of the national high-debt situation and offer quick-fix solutions. These firms manage to get nonprofit status, which confuses the consumer even more because he or she does not know how to distinguish a legitimate agency from an abusive one.

Legitimate credit counseling firms will meet or talk with their clients, review their finances, and recommend a budget and/or debt payment plan. Fees are generally nominal or there are none at all. If you initially see that the service is free but later learn there is a "donation cost" or other significant expense for every service, consider this a warning sign.

Rather than include an exhaustive, ever-changing list of organizations and services, I am recommending you do a search on *www.google.com* or any other favorite search engine. Start with "financial counseling" or "debt management" for your key word search.

Below are three national organizations with an established history:

National Foundation for Credit Counseling (NFCC)
www.nfcc.org; 800-388-2227

NFCC is the nation's oldest, largest, and longest-serving nonprofit credit counseling network, setting the national standard for quality credit counseling, debt reduction services, and education for financial wellness. Member agencies around the country, often known as the Consumer Credit Counseling Service (CCCS) or other names, can be identified by the NFCC member seal. Their seal signifies high standards for agency accreditation, counselor certification, and policies that ensure confidential services. Their programs are designed to help you make one payment, get debt paid off early, and reduce the amount of monthly creditor payments, often by negotiating for reduced or eliminated finance charges and other fees.

Association of Independent Consumer Credit Counseling Agencies (AICCCA)
www.aiccca.org; 800-703-8787

AICCCA is a national membership organization representing nonprofit credit counseling companies that provide consumer credit counseling, debt management, and financial education services. The AICCCA provides services designed to establish balance among consumers, creditors, and member agencies for the successful rehabilitation of debt-challenged families and individuals. Before working with any nonprofit organization, be sure it is a member of either the NFCC or AICCCA.

As valuable as these services can be, I want you to be aware of the *possible negative effect they could have on your credit report.* In the long run, you will have to weigh the long-term pros and cons of having significant help with paying off your debt and the impact on your credit score. For some people, their credit score is already so low due to their debt that their primary focus is just on getting help with their debt situation.

continued on next page

GETTING ONLINE HELP FOR DEBT continued

Association for Financial Counseling and Planning Education (AFCPE)

www.afcpe.org; (614) 485-9650

AFCPE is a professional organization that supports and promotes the field of financial counseling and planning education. The membership consists of university and cooperative extension educators, military financial counselors, private practitioners, and interest organizations and government officials.

Getting help from a financial counselor (whether through an organization or privately) can be invaluable to help you improve your financial situation and your emotional and mental state. Ask about their background training and accreditation. If possible, find someone who is certified as an accredited financial counselor (AFC) through AFCPE.

Debt Repayment Worksheet

Once you have completed the top part of the **Debt Payoff Record** on pages 101–103 and outlined all of your debt, it may be overwhelming to stop and see the total amount of debt to be paid off. If you are in a situation where there is not enough disposable money each month to even pay the monthly minimums, and you are determined to pay back your debt in full, know that there is a solution.

The **Debt Repayment Worksheet** on page 115 is provided to help when you are *in a very tight financial situation and* **choose not to declare bankruptcy or use the services of any nonprofit credit counseling agency**. This approach will take time and patience. The payoff, however, will be preservation of your personal and financial integrity.

This repayment concept has been discussed and outlined very thoroughly in Jerrold Mundis's *How to Get Out of Debt, Stay Out of Debt and Live Prosperously* and Dave Ramsey's *The Financial PeacePlanner* books. I would highly recommend you review these books if you choose this route. The **Debt Repayment Worksheet** summarizes how to work out a *fair share repayment plan* for all of your creditors using what disposable money you have available to pay off your debt.

How to Use this Worksheet

First, fill out your **Monthly Budget Worksheet** (starting on page 70) so you know exactly how much your monthly bills and expenses are. Next, determine how much money you can use to pay toward your debt. With this figure and your total balances from the **Debt Payoff Record** beginning on page 101, we will work out each creditor's percentage and the amount of money you have available for paying them.

Now looking at the **Debt Repayment Worksheet** on page 115, start with your "Balance Due" for each creditor. Divide this by your "Total Combined Debt" (from the **Debt Payoff Record**) to find out the "Share Percent" to pay to that creditor. This means each creditor is being paid based on a percentage to keep your payments consistent and fairly divided among all the creditors. You are paying the creditor an amount that represents a *fair "share percent" of your total overall debt*, versus what the creditor may be requiring.

Next, multiply that "Share Percent" by the available "Disposable Income" (from working out the **Monthly Budget Worksheet** on page 70) to determine your new monthly payment to each creditor.

To make this method work, there are four things you need to do:

1. Contact each creditor and explain your plan by including a copy of your budget, the first payment check, and this outline of debt repayment.
2. Stay honest and stick to your commitment religiously, and make every one of these monthly payments on time.
3. Track and manage your spending diligently (use the **Monthly Expense Record** worksheets, starting on page 126).
4. Do not incur any new debt.

It also doesn't hurt to *pray* in your own way!

During this repayment period, it will also be important to find ways to raise some extra cash to pay toward your debt or to cover the surprise incidentals that come up, whether through selling items, holding yard sales, working overtime, or getting part-time work. Apply any extra money from gifts, rebates, or refunds toward this debt. In the future, you will have the opportunity again to treat yourself with that gift money. For now you are trading a piece of furniture or jewelry for some peace of mind.

If your creditors resist the nominal payment amounts (for example, they are asking for payments of $100 and you are sending $35), remind them you are doing this to avoid bankruptcy and persist with your program and keep making payments. Hold the goal of being debt-free and keep knowing that you can pay off your debt slowly and methodically. Continue to explain and show your plan and follow through with it.

You can't be forced to pay money you do not have. This system will give you the strength to resist aggressive creditors. If you pay more than planned to one aggressive creditor, the whole repayment plan will go out of balance, and you will be back in the familiar discouraging debt cycle again.

Keep in mind this financial condition will eventually pass. Amazingly, you will find that these initial small amounts of payments start to increase as you slowly begin to pay off debt and work with a program. As each creditor gets paid in full over time, *recalculate the balance due and the total combined debt*. Increase your payments accordingly, and you will start to see those balances go down. Stop and realize that you are now getting *out of debt* instead of into debt, and notice how you are starting to regain a solid sense of control in your life once again.

As Winston Churchill once said: "Never, never, never give up!"

DEBT REPAYMENT WORKSHEET

Step 1 Disposable Income*

Total Amount of Disposable Income Available to Pay Off Debt: $_____

(Calculate your budget on the **Monthly Budget Worksheet** beginning on page 70.)

How much money is available to apply to debt?

The more you owe a creditor, the more money and higher percent you will pay them from your Disposable Income.

Step 2 Total Combined Debt**

Total Amount of All Debt Combined: $_____

(Transfer the total from the **Debt Payoff Record** beginning on page 101.)

Step 3 New Payment ***

List below the total balances you owe each creditor listed on the **Debt Payoff Record**. Start with the smallest balance and then follow the formula below to determine the new payment for each creditor.

Creditor	Balance Due	÷	Total** Combined Debt	=	Share Percent (of Total Combined Debt)	×	Disposable* Income	=	New Payment***
Dentist	$ 500	÷	$11,500	=	4.3%	×	$700	=	$30.43
Visa	$1,500	÷	$11,500	=	13.0%	×	$700	=	$91.30

Credit Card
Purchase Record

To avoid a shocking bill at the end of the month, if you are still managing your finances manually versus online, keep careful track of your credit card charges. This way, you can anticipate what the bill will be and prepare for it by making the appropriate adjustments in your spending and your planning.

By knowing the status of your charges at all times, you become much more selective and careful about impulse charging. When you reach this point, you know that you have learned how to keep from getting overextended and have taken one more step toward controlling your finances.

How to Use this Chart

First find out and enter the "Billing Cycle Closing Date." ① Call each credit card company and ask them what this date is for your account. By knowing this information, you can manage your charges and payments more proactively instead of unconsciously. Then record all charges ② made during the month until that date so you know which purchases will be included on that month's upcoming bill. Purchases charged after that closing date should be entered in the next month's column (the month for which you actually will be billed). Jot down in the corner the date you made the charge. ③

Remember, this chart is flexible. If you use different cards frequently, draw one or two lines across both pages to create new sections for different cards. You can also carry an extra check register with you to record your charges for other cards. Make the chart work for you!

CREDIT CARD PURCHASE RECORD

SAMPLE

	JAN.		FEB.		MAR.		APR.		MAY		JUNE
Billing Cycle Closing Date: ① _____		_____		_____		_____		_____		_____	
Item	Amount	Item	Amount	Item	Amount	Item	Amount	Item	Amount	Item	Amount
3/gas ②	14.91										
7/Shoes	20.82										
Total											

③

ONLINE/ELECTRONIC CONNECTION TO *THE BUDGET KIT*

Online Bill Payments

If you don't want to list your charges on this worksheet, you can register online at your credit card company's website and see your current charges and balance due. As you fill in the "Installment" blanks of the **Monthly Budget Worksheet** to plan out your bills, you will know exactly how much to anticipate for your credit card payments. When your bill arrives, you can still pay by check or pay the bill directly online from your checking account, using either the credit card website or your bank's website.

Online Budget Programs

Coordinating credit card charges with a monthly budget accurately and effectively is probably one of the more challenging steps depending on your online budget program, credit card debt situation, and level of sophistication. Even the manual approach to this process gets confusing for many people. See if your online budget program has a way to link a credit card charge in a particular category with the same category in your outlined budget for the month and then has a way to plan the payment. Not all programs are designed to coordinate this process.

The more popular online budget programs like Finicity Money Manager—Mvelopes® and Quicken (Mint) will have well-designed systems for virtually coordinating the credit card charges with the monthly budget and then including a virtual transfer for the payment plan. If you are a heavy credit card user, be sure this feature is offered with the online program you are using and is easy to use.

CREDIT CARD PURCHASE RECORD

JAN.		FEB.		MAR.		APR.		MAY		JUNE	
Billing Cycle Closing Date: _____		_____		_____		_____		_____		_____	
Item	Amount	Item	Amount	Item	Amount	Item	Amount	Item	Amount	Item	Amount
Total											

CREDIT CARD PURCHASE RECORD

JULY		AUG.		SEPT.		OCT.		NOV.		DEC.	
Billing Cycle Closing Date: _____		_____		_____		_____		_____		_____	
Item	Amount	Item	Amount	Item	Amount	Item	Amount	Item	Amount	Item	Amount
Total											

Monthly Expense Record

Sometimes it takes the black-and-white approach to get someone's attention. Connie started using the workbook to track expenses and plan ahead when she and her husband knew they would be retiring in a few years. Her husband was staggered when he saw the expenses they both spent for six months. He was finally ready to sit down and outline and plan the finances together with Connie. They also successfully started saving for their travel plans. The workbook became an effective communication tool—a way for getting out of the dream world and back into reality.

Finding Out Where All the Money Goes

How many times have you asked yourself, "Where did all the money go?" Even keeping detailed records in the check register or reviewing the bank statements and credit card statements doesn't always give a clear answer to that question. With these worksheets and with some firm self-discipline, you will easily and very graphically know in a more organized way exactly where all your money has gone as well as how much money has come in.

Begin by picking a time every day to jot down all the spending for that day. Some people like to carry a small notebook or use their mobile devices to record all their daily cash in a more organized way. Others carry this workbook or these sheets in their car, backpack, or briefcase and record as they go. With practice and determination, you will develop the habit of regularly recording all *cash, debits, checks,* and *charged* expenses. At first this may seem time-consuming and uncomfortable. However, once you get past the 21-day marker for creating a new habit, you will notice that your recording literally takes only minutes a day.

Be patient with yourself and the results. The first month or two, your numbers may not be perfect, but the habit is being developed and information is emerging. By the third month or earlier, you will be amazed at the results and the shift in your attitude.

"All of a sudden, miraculously, my husband is on board with my desperation to budget!! When I showed him that his ATM withdrawals are more than $800 a month and the nonbank ATM fees and

overdrafts are another $400 per month, he went absolutely white as a ghost. I think he's got the idea, and we were both able to sit and talk. I went over the monthly automatic deductions with him, and we minimized all we can."

—Linda F., MBA, AZ

Using this worksheet will have a total multisensory impact, subconsciously, on your spending. Kinesthetically, you are manually writing down each expense. Recording daily, versus recording a basketful of receipts at the end of each week or month, will give you more valuable input than you realize. Visually, you are taking the information in and noticing all the other entries in the column above. You are starting to note all the money spent to date and probably thinking you want to cut back. And then when you start talking to your partner or to yourself about the expenses, you are engaging the auditory senses. All of these senses combined are changing the way you manage and handle your money.

Ultimately, your payoff will be the sense of control you have over your finances and finally being aware of your overall spending. Many people insist that once they began tracking their spending, they started spending less and saving more. In fact, one reader, Margaret, said, "Probably the most surprising lesson for me was to see that it really is the *small* daily choices that drive the big financial picture."

Recording how cash is spent is important. Every time you write a check for cash or use the automated teller machine (ATM), write down where you actually spend that cash. Itemizing all the cash provides more valuable information for you than just recording "$50 cash" or "misc." six times as an expense and not really knowing how it was spent or where the money went.

Debit cards and ATMs as conveniences can be either a blessing or a curse depending on how you use them. After months of total chaos and overdraft charges in the checking account, one couple worked out their monthly budget to determine exactly how much cash was needed each week. On Mondays Joe gets his lump cash and knows it has to cover his gas, coffee, meals, snacks, and all other incidentals for the week. Ginny sticks with the checkbook. Both are relieved to finally always know their current balance in the checkbook.

If you seem to have more month than money most of the time, remember your choices. You can reduce, postpone, modify, or eliminate your spending. If you are not sure where to begin, a review of these filled-out worksheets will quickly show you which optional categories to start with. Maybe you need to do more of your own home or car repairs, be more energy-conscious, eat out less, take your lunch and beverages to work, cut back on gifts, start carpooling, or do whatever fits your abilities and interests. When you do cut back, the results will be noticed immediately.

As you work with these worksheets, modify them to fit your unique life-style. The expense categories, net income, savings, investment, and retirement sections serve as guidelines to set up your own system.

"I like using a color code like a highlighter or some key symbols to designate where the money came from to pay for certain expenses. It helps me know when I used money from our reserve account or household savings account. That way I feel I'm working with a plan and can see how the extra expenses are planned and covered."

If you have *tax-deductible expenses, note them here.* If you want all you tax records kept together, you can use the handy **Tax-Deductible Expense Record** in Part Three.

You will notice the emphasis on *net income*, not on gross income, through-out this workbook. The idea is to deal only with the actual income that is deposited in your account and not record more information than you need to. The gross income information is usually on your check stubs. If you need to keep a record of your taxes, FICA, retirement savings, and other deductions, you can use the "End-of-the-Year Tax Information" section on the bottom of the **Summary-for-the-Year Record** worksheet following these monthly expense pages.

Do You *Really* Have to Track *All* Those Expenses?

After discussing the advantages of tracking personal spending and having a plan, it's also fair to mention that this system doesn't always fit all personal temperaments and lifestyles. What is important is that everyone has *some system that helps them manage their finances wisely and gives them a sense of financial control.*

I have a good friend, Rick, who has his own system. He and his wife are conservative spenders, pay their credit cards off in full each month, and man-age their finances well. They don't use an official budget or track any house-hold expenses. Not only do they not utilize any online bank accounts, but he and his wife (and boys) don't even own cell phones. They do, however, use bank withdrawals for most of their bills.

One time, while watching him go through all the monthly household receipts, checking them off against the credit card statements, I became curi-ous if he ever found any errors. Nope. Not in all the years he had been going through the ritual had he found one error. Now, one could say that whole routine was quite a waste of time (which I have to admit did cross my mind). However, here's the real point. Rick's comment was very telling: "I find it very peaceful to go through all the statements and check off each receipt."

This routine was actually helping Rick tangibly stay in touch with all the household finances. And as he said, it was giving him much peace of mind. I find that many of us function better with the comfort and security of routines. Since each credit card had a specific purpose (one for groceries and gas, another for medical, and the third for covering the balance of household/personal spending), he really did have a system that worked for him and kept him on top of the household spending.

The real point is finding what works best for you in terms of being able to pay all bills in full and on time, continuing to add money to savings and investments, having minimal debt, and living mindfully so *you* ultimately have financial peace of mind.

THE ONLINE/ELECTRONIC CONNECTION TO *THE BUDGET KIT*

Electronic Tracking Systems

The **Monthly Expense Record** is actually a very effective tool to use as a guideline for setting up any electronic tracking system and understanding the basic concept behind the tracking. Over the years, people have called telling me how they preferred the organization and the categories from this worksheet to the categories in the personal finance software package they were using. Instead of organizing the spending categories alphabetically, this worksheet was designed around the actual spending styles of thousands of readers and clients.

Whether you use a worksheet you created yourself; use a personal finance software program like Quicken, MoneyDance®, AceMoney (see Web addresses below), or another online budget system (see Web addresses below); or have explored different apps for your smartphone, you can utilize the most helpful aspects of this worksheet as you transition to electronic tracking.

The key with any system is interacting directly with all your spending transactions. This will keep you from going into automatic pilot with your daily spending and help you stay more in touch with your overall financial situation.

The Internet is exploding with so many personal finance resources, it's hard to know what new programs (like the mobile apps) will emerge or what current products and websites will still be in existence in a few years. Even many of the larger banks and credit card companies offer some pretty compelling free money manager/budgeting online programs as part of their services.

As of this writing, the following resources and websites seem to be the most stable and recognized. Your best bet is to do a Google search for "personal finance software" or "Web-based personal finance software" reviews. You can also check out *http://personal-finance-software-review.toptenreviews.com* (software programs) or *http://financialsoft.about.com/od/morefinancialsoftware/tp/Online_Software_List. htm* (online/Web-based programs).

Below are a few of the more popular current programs.

Personal Finance Software:	**Online Personal Finance Software:**
http://quicken.intuit.com	*www.mint.com*
http://moneydance.com	*www.finicity.com*
www.mechcad.net/products/acemoney	*https://money.strands.com*

Monthly Expense Record Worksheet on Excel

If you're not quite ready to move over to a total personal finance software program or online budget system just yet, but do feel comfortable using Excel, there is another option. The worksheets on the following pages are part of the core worksheets available on Excel. These are available at *http://moneytracker. com/books-TheBudgetKitExcel.htm*. Currently, there is still a small fee. The worksheets look exactly the same way on the screen as on these pages and have the added convenience of doing all the calculations for you. There are separate tabs on the bottom for every month and then a Summary for the Year that is automatically totaling every time you enter an expense. Here again, I recommend starting out manually with the workbook for a month or so because of the advantages mentioned earlier.

MONTHLY EXPENSE RECORD

Balance Forward from Last Month:
Cash: $37.00   Checking: $435.00   Savings: $11,796.45

NET INCOME

SALARY/COMMISSIONS	Chris	Kim	TOTAL
Jobs	1,280	1,707	2,987
Jobs		1,707	1,707
		TOTAL INCOME	4,694
OTHER			
Yard sale (wasn't planned, but came in handy)			50
From Reserve Savings for this month's expenses			1,320
Left over from last month			435
		Subtotal Other Income	1,805
		TOTAL NET INCOME	6,499

SAVINGS

(Describe)	
Reserve (pulled $1,320 for September expenses)	1,114
Goals	75
Emergency	115
TOTAL SAVINGS	1,304

INVESTMENTS/RETIREMENT

(See Payroll Deduction)	
TOTAL INVESTMENTS/RETIREMENT	

Expense Detail

		FOOD		HOUSEHOLD				TRANSPORTATION			PERSONAL		HEALTH	
	groceries	cafeteria fast food dining out school lunches	tobacco alcohol snacks beverages water	cleaner mainten. house yard pool	appliances furniture furnishings supplies	postage copies ATM fees bank fees misc.	interest taxes	gas	auto mainten. wash license	taxi transit tolls/passes parking	clothing alterations dry clean. laundry shoe care	toiletries cosmetics hair nails massage	doctor dentist vision medicine vitamins	personal growth therapy
1	40	15						14						
2		8		20										
3	36							9						65
4			15						15				20	
5		29												
6			5					13						
7	44		6									15		
8														
9	67	8			20						44			
10								15						
11	17	14										10		
12			5										13	
13			5						100	DMV				
14			6											
15	11													
16		12						10			21			
17														
18	29	8	5	26								Hair		
19												80		
20	10										14			
21					23									65
22			11					15						
23				10										
24													15	
25	150													
26		7	6					9			15			
27						9								
28	32													
29														
30	67	27						20						
31	18													
T*	521	128	64	56	43	9	—	105	115	—	109	90	48	130
B*	550	155	40	45	50	10		125	100		110	80	35	130
D*	29	27	(24)	(11)	7	1	0	20	(15)	0	1	(10)	(13)	0

Weeks: rows 1–7 = WEEK 1; rows 8–14 = WEEK 2; rows 15–21 = WEEK 3; rows 22–31 = WEEK 4

* T = Total; B = Budget; D = Difference

MONTHLY EXPENSE RECORD

FIXED EXPENSES

Monthly	Amount	Monthly	Amount
Mortgage/Rent	984	Insurance:	
Assn. Fee		House/Apt	
Heating Oil/Gas	45	Auto (SUV & Truck)	925
Electricity	75	Life	
Water/Refuse	35	Health	
Garbage/Sewer	65	Dental	
Telephone	29	Disability	
Cellular Phone	59	Long Term	
Cable/Satellite/TiVo	60		
Internet	49		
Child Support		Storage	
Spousal Support		Health Club	25
		TOTAL FIXED EXPENSES	2,351

INSTALLMENT EXPENSES

Loans/Credit Cards	Amount
Visa	100
MC	200
Student Loan	167
Car Payment	291
TOTAL	758

TOTAL EXPENSES

Total Fixed Expenses	2,351
Total Installment Expenses	758
Total Monthly Expenses from Below	2,065
GRAND TOTAL EXPENSES	5,174
Plus Amount Paid to Savings 1,304	6,478

Difference: TOTAL INCOME — GRAND TOTAL = $21

	RECREATION/ENTERTAINMENT/EDUCATION						FAMILY			GENERAL				
	vacation trips	entertain. DVD movies music parties	lottery sports hobbies lessons clubs	computer upgrades software supplies service	seminar workshop tuition supplies	newspaper books magazines software games/apps	elder care child care sitter tutor	infant exp. allowance school exp. toys arcades	pet vet supplies services sitter	gifts cards flowers	charitable contribut. church temple	work expense dues reimburse-ments	prof. services legal CPA investment	other (add explanation)
WEEK 1 — 1														Mad $
2		9						School			50			50
3								75						
4						5								
5														
6														
7								20			50			
WEEK 2 — 8														
9														
10														
11														
12						15								
13														
14		Season Tix												
WEEK 3 — 15		75												
16											50			
17								20						
18														
19						24					50			
20										10				
21														
WEEK 4 — 22			21											
23						19								
24														
25								5			50			
26														
27														
28														
29											50			
30														
31														
T*	—	84	—	21	—	63	—	120	—	10	300	—	—	50
B*		100				65		115			300			50
D*	0	16	0	0	0	2	0	(5)	0	(10)	0	0	0	0

* T = Total; B = Budget; D = Difference

MONTHLY EXPENSE RECORD

Balance Forward from Last Month:

Cash: _____ Checking: _____ Savings: _____

NET INCOME

			TOTAL
SALARY/COMMISSIONS			
TOTAL INCOME			
OTHER			
Subtotal Other Income			
TOTAL NET INCOME			

SAVINGS

(Describe)	
TOTAL SAVINGS	

INVESTMENTS/RETIREMENT

TOTAL INVESTMENTS/RETIREMENT	

		FOOD		HOUSEHOLD				TRANSPORTATION			PERSONAL		HEALTH	
	groceries	cafeteria fast food dining out school lunches	tobacco alcohol snacks beverages water	cleaner mainten. house yard pool	appliances furniture furnishings supplies	postage copies ATM fees bank fees misc.	interest taxes	gas	auto mainten. wash license	taxi transit tolls/passes parking	clothing alterations dry clean. laundry shoe care	toiletries cosmetics hair nails massage	doctor dentist vision medicine vitamins	personal growth therapy
WEEK 1 1 2 3 4 5 6 7														
WEEK 2 8 9 10 11 12 13 14														
WEEK 3 15 16 17 18 19 20 21														
WEEK 4 22 23 24 25 26 27 28 29 30 31														
T*														
B*														
D*														

* T = Total; B = Budget; D = Difference

MONTHLY EXPENSE RECORD

FIXED EXPENSES

Monthly	Amount	Monthly	Amount
Mortgage/Rent		Insurance:	
Assn. Fee		House/Apt	
Heating Oil/Gas		Auto	
Electricity		Life	
Water/Refuse		Health	
Garbage/Sewer		Dental	
Telephone		Disability	
Cellular Phone		Long Term	
Cable/Satellite/TiVo			
Internet			
Child Support			
Spousal Support			
		TOTAL FIXED EXPENSES	

INSTALLMENT EXPENSES

Loans/Credit Cards	Amount
TOTAL	

TOTAL EXPENSES

Total Fixed Expenses	
Total Installment Expenses	
Total Monthly Expenses from Below	
GRAND TOTAL EXPENSES	
Plus Amount Paid to Savings	

	RECREATION/ENTERTAINMENT/EDUCATION						FAMILY			GENERAL				
	vacation trips	entertain. DVD movies music parties	lottery sports hobbies lessons clubs	computer upgrades software supplies service	seminar workshop tuition supplies	newspaper books magazines software games/apps	elder care child care sitter tutor	infant exp. allowance school exp. toys arcades	pet vet supplies services sitter	gifts cards flowers	charitable contribut. church temple	work expense dues reimburse-ments	prof. services legal CPA investment	other (add explanation)
WEEK 1 — 1														
2														
3														
4														
5														
6														
7														
WEEK 2 — 8														
9														
10														
11														
12														
13														
14														
WEEK 3 — 15														
16														
17														
18														
19														
20														
21														
22														
23														
24														
WEEK 4 — 25														
26														
27														
28														
29														
30														
31														
T*														
B*														
D*														

* T = Total; B = Budget; D = Difference

MONTHLY EXPENSE RECORD

Balance Forward from Last Month:

Cash: _____ Checking: _____ Savings: _____

NET INCOME

			TOTAL
SALARY/COMMISSIONS			
		TOTAL INCOME	
OTHER			
		Subtotal Other Income	
		TOTAL NET INCOME	

SAVINGS

(Describe)	
TOTAL SAVINGS	

INVESTMENTS/RETIREMENT

TOTAL INVESTMENTS/RETIREMENT	

		FOOD			HOUSEHOLD				TRANSPORTATION			PERSONAL		HEALTH	
	groceries	cafeteria fast food dining out school lunches	tobacco alcohol snacks beverages water	cleaner mainten. house yard pool	appliances furniture furnishings supplies	postage copies ATM fees bank fees misc.	interest taxes	gas	auto mainten. wash license	taxi transit tolls/passes parking	clothing alterations dry clean. laundry shoe care	toiletries cosmetics hair nails massage	doctor dentist vision medicine vitamins	personal growth therapy
WEEK 1 — 1														
2														
3														
4														
5														
6														
7														
WEEK 2 — 8														
9														
10														
11														
12														
13														
14														
WEEK 3 — 15														
16														
17														
18														
19														
20														
21														
WEEK 4 — 22														
23														
24														
25														
26														
27														
28														
29														
30														
31														
T*														
B*														
D*														

* T = Total; B = Budget; D = Difference

MONTHLY EXPENSE RECORD

FIXED EXPENSES

Monthly	Amount	Monthly	Amount
Mortgage/Rent		Insurance:	
Assn. Fee		House/Apt	
Heating Oil/Gas		Auto	
Electricity		Life	
Water/Refuse		Health	
Garbage/Sewer		Dental	
Telephone		Disability	
Cellular Phone		Long Term	
Cable/Satellite/TiVo			
Internet			
Child Support			
Spousal Support			
TOTAL FIXED EXPENSES			

INSTALLMENT EXPENSES

Loans/Credit Cards	Amount
TOTAL	

TOTAL EXPENSES

Total Fixed Expenses	
Total Installment Expenses	
Total Monthly Expenses from Below	
GRAND TOTAL EXPENSES	
Plus Amount Paid to Savings	

	RECREATION/ENTERTAINMENT/EDUCATION						FAMILY			GENERAL					
	vacation trips	entertain. DVD movies music parties	lottery sports hobbies lessons clubs	computer upgrades software supplies service	seminar workshop tuition supplies	newspaper books magazines software games/apps	elder care child care sitter tutor	infant exp. allowance school exp. toys arcades	pet vet supplies services sitter	gifts cards flowers	charitable contribut. church temple	work expense dues reimburse-ments	prof. services legal CPA investment	other (add explanation)
WEEK 1 1–7														
WEEK 2 8–14														
WEEK 3 15–21														
WEEK 4 22–31														
T*														
B*														
D*														

* T = Total; B = Budget; D = Difference

MONTHLY EXPENSE RECORD

Balance Forward from Last Month:
Cash: _____ Checking: _____ Savings: _____

NET INCOME

			TOTAL
SALARY/COMMISSIONS			
		TOTAL INCOME	
OTHER			
		Subtotal Other Income	
		TOTAL NET INCOME	

SAVINGS

(Describe)	
TOTAL SAVINGS	

INVESTMENTS/RETIREMENT

TOTAL INVESTMENTS/RETIREMENT	

	FOOD			HOUSEHOLD				TRANSPORTATION			PERSONAL		HEALTH	
	groceries	cafeteria fast food dining out school lunches	tobacco alcohol snacks beverages water	cleaner mainten. house yard pool	appliances furniture furnishings supplies	postage copies ATM fees bank fees misc.	interest taxes	gas	auto mainten. wash license	taxi transit tolls/passes parking	clothing alterations dry clean. laundry shoe care	toiletries cosmetics hair nails massage	doctor dentist vision medicine vitamins	personal growth therapy
WEEK 1 1														
2														
3														
4														
5														
6														
7														
WEEK 2 8														
9														
10														
11														
12														
13														
14														
WEEK 3 15														
16														
17														
18														
19														
20														
21														
WEEK 4 22														
23														
24														
25														
26														
27														
28														
29														
30														
31														
T*														
B*														
D*														

* T = Total; B = Budget; D = Difference

MONTHLY EXPENSE RECORD

FIXED EXPENSES

Monthly	Amount	Monthly	Amount
Mortgage/Rent		Insurance:	
Assn. Fee		House/Apt	
Heating Oil/Gas		Auto	
Electricity		Life	
Water/Refuse		Health	
Garbage/Sewer		Dental	
Telephone		Disability	
Cellular Phone		Long Term	
Cable/Satellite/TiVo			
Internet			
Child Support			
Spousal Support			
		TOTAL FIXED EXPENSES	

INSTALLMENT EXPENSES

Loans/Credit Cards	Amount
TOTAL	

TOTAL EXPENSES

Total Fixed Expenses	
Total Installment Expenses	
Total Monthly Expenses from Below	
GRAND TOTAL EXPENSES	
Plus Amount Paid to Savings	

		RECREATION/ENTERTAINMENT/EDUCATION					FAMILY			GENERAL				
	vacation trips	entertain. DVD movies music parties	lottery sports hobbies lessons clubs	computer upgrades software supplies service	seminar workshop tuition supplies	newspaper books magazines software games/apps	elder care child care sitter tutor	infant exp. allowance school exp. toys arcades	pet vet supplies services sitter	gifts cards flowers	charitable contribut. church temple	work expense dues reimburse-ments	prof. services legal CPA investment	other (add explanation)
WEEK 1 — 1														
2														
3														
4														
5														
6														
7														
WEEK 2 — 8														
9														
10														
11														
12														
13														
14														
WEEK 3 — 15														
16														
17														
18														
19														
20														
21														
WEEK 4 — 22														
23														
24														
25														
26														
27														
28														
29														
30														
31														
T*														
B*														
D*														

* T = Total; B = Budget; D = Difference

MONTHLY EXPENSE RECORD

Cash: _____ Checking: _____ Savings: _____

NET INCOME

			TOTAL
SALARY/COMMISSIONS			
		TOTAL INCOME	
OTHER			
		Subtotal Other Income	
		TOTAL NET INCOME	

SAVINGS

(Describe)	
TOTAL SAVINGS	

INVESTMENTS/RETIREMENT

TOTAL INVESTMENTS/RETIREMENT	

	FOOD			HOUSEHOLD				TRANSPORTATION			PERSONAL		HEALTH	
	groceries	cafeteria fast food dining out school lunches	tobacco alcohol snacks beverages water	cleaner mainten. house yard pool	appliances furniture furnishings supplies	postage copies ATM fees bank fees misc.	interest taxes	gas	auto mainten. wash license	taxi transit tolls/passes parking	clothing alterations dry clean. laundry shoe care	toiletries cosmetics hair nails massage	doctor dentist vision medicine vitamins	personal growth therapy
WEEK 1 — 1														
2														
3														
4														
5														
6														
7														
WEEK 2 — 8														
9														
10														
11														
12														
13														
14														
WEEK 3 — 15														
16														
17														
18														
19														
20														
21														
22														
23														
24														
WEEK 4 — 25														
26														
27														
28														
29														
30														
31														
T*														
B*														
D*														

* T = Total; B = Budget; D = Difference

MONTHLY EXPENSE RECORD

FIXED EXPENSES

Monthly	Amount	Monthly	Amount
Mortgage/Rent		Insurance:	
Assn. Fee		House/Apt	
Heating Oil/Gas		Auto	
Electricity		Life	
Water/Refuse		Health	
Garbage/Sewer		Dental	
Telephone		Disability	
Cellular Phone		Long Term	
Cable/Satellite/TiVo			
Internet			
Child Support			
Spousal Support			
		TOTAL FIXED EXPENSES	

INSTALLMENT EXPENSES

Loans/Credit Cards	Amount
TOTAL	

TOTAL EXPENSES

Total Fixed Expenses	
Total Installment Expenses	
Total Monthly Expenses from Below	
GRAND TOTAL EXPENSES	
Plus Amount Paid to Savings	

	RECREATION/ENTERTAINMENT/EDUCATION						FAMILY			GENERAL				
	vacation trips	entertain. DVD movies music parties	lottery sports hobbies lessons clubs	computer upgrades software supplies service	seminar workshop tuition supplies	newspaper books magazines software games/apps	elder care child care sitter tutor	infant exp. allowance school exp. toys arcades	pet vet supplies services sitter	gifts cards flowers	charitable contribut. church temple	work expense dues reimburse-ments	prof. services legal CPA investment	other (add explanation)
WEEK 1 — 1														
2														
3														
4														
5														
6														
7														
WEEK 2 — 8														
9														
10														
11														
12														
13														
14														
WEEK 3 — 15														
16														
17														
18														
19														
20														
21														
22														
23														
24														
WEEK 4 — 25														
26														
27														
28														
29														
30														
31														
T*														
B*														
D*														

* T = Total; B = Budget; D = Difference

MONTHLY EXPENSE RECORD

Balance Forward from Last Month:

Cash: _____   Checking: _____   Savings: _____

NET INCOME

			TOTAL
SALARY/COMMISSIONS			
TOTAL INCOME			
OTHER			
Subtotal Other Income			
TOTAL NET INCOME			

SAVINGS

(Describe)	
TOTAL SAVINGS	

INVESTMENTS/RETIREMENT

TOTAL INVESTMENTS/RETIREMENT	

		FOOD			HOUSEHOLD				TRANSPORTATION			PERSONAL		HEALTH	
		groceries	cafeteria fast food dining out school lunches	tobacco alcohol snacks beverages water	cleaner mainten. house yard pool	appliances furniture furnishings supplies	postage copies ATM fees bank fees misc.	interest taxes	gas	auto mainten. wash license	taxi transit tolls/passes parking	clothing alterations dry clean. laundry shoe care	toiletries cosmetics hair nails massage	doctor dentist vision medicine vitamins	personal growth therapy
WEEK 1	1														
	2														
	3														
	4														
	5														
	6														
	7														
WEEK 2	8														
	9														
	10														
	11														
	12														
	13														
	14														
WEEK 3	15														
	16														
	17														
	18														
	19														
	20														
	21														
WEEK 4	22														
	23														
	24														
	25														
	26														
	27														
	28														
	29														
	30														
	31														
	T*														
	B*														
	D*														

* T = Total; B = Budget; D = Difference

MONTHLY EXPENSE RECORD

FIXED EXPENSES

Monthly	Amount	Monthly	Amount
Mortgage/Rent		Insurance:	
Assn. Fee		House/Apt	
Heating Oil/Gas		Auto	
Electricity		Life	
Water/Refuse		Health	
Garbage/Sewer		Dental	
Telephone		Disability	
Cellular Phone		Long Term	
Cable/Satellite/TiVo			
Internet			
Child Support			
Spousal Support			
TOTAL FIXED EXPENSES			

INSTALLMENT EXPENSES

Loans/Credit Cards	Amount
TOTAL	

TOTAL EXPENSES

Total Fixed Expenses	
Total Installment Expenses	
Total Monthly Expenses from Below	
GRAND TOTAL EXPENSES	
Plus Amount Paid to Savings	

RECREATION/ENTERTAINMENT/EDUCATION — FAMILY — GENERAL

	vacation trips	entertain. DVD movies music parties	lottery sports hobbies lessons clubs	computer upgrades software supplies service	seminar workshop tuition supplies	newspaper books magazines software games/apps	elder care child care sitter tutor	infant exp. allowance school exp. toys arcades	pet vet supplies services sitter	gifts cards flowers	charitable contribut. church temple	work expense dues reimburse-ments	prof. services legal CPA investment	other (add explanation)
WEEK 1 1														
2														
3														
4														
5														
6														
7														
WEEK 2 8														
9														
10														
11														
12														
13														
14														
WEEK 3 15														
16														
17														
18														
19														
20														
21														
WEEK 4 22														
23														
24														
25														
26														
27														
28														
29														
30														
31														
T*														
B*														
D*														

* T = Total; B = Budget; D = Difference

MONTHLY EXPENSE RECORD

Balance Forward from Last Month:

Cash: _____ Checking: _____ Savings: _____

NET INCOME

			TOTAL
SALARY/COMMISSIONS			
		TOTAL INCOME	
OTHER			
		Subtotal Other Income	
		TOTAL NET INCOME	

SAVINGS

(Describe)	
TOTAL SAVINGS	

INVESTMENTS/RETIREMENT

TOTAL INVESTMENTS/RETIREMENT	

		FOOD		HOUSEHOLD				TRANSPORTATION			PERSONAL		HEALTH	
	groceries	cafeteria fast food dining out school lunches	tobacco alcohol snacks beverages water	cleaner mainten. house yard pool	appliances furniture furnishings supplies	postage copies ATM fees bank fees misc.	interest taxes	gas	auto mainten. wash license	taxi transit tolls/passes parking	clothing alterations dry clean. laundry shoe care	toiletries cosmetics hair nails massage	doctor dentist vision medicine vitamins	personal growth therapy
WEEK 1 — 1														
2														
3														
4														
5														
6														
7														
WEEK 2 — 8														
9														
10														
11														
12														
13														
14														
WEEK 3 — 15														
16														
17														
18														
19														
20														
21														
WEEK 4 — 22														
23														
24														
25														
26														
27														
28														
29														
30														
31														
T*														
B*														
D*														

* T = Total; B = Budget; D = Difference

MONTHLY EXPENSE RECORD

FIXED EXPENSES

Monthly	Amount	Monthly	Amount
Mortgage/Rent		Insurance:	
Assn. Fee		House/Apt	
Heating Oil/Gas		Auto	
Electricity		Life	
Water/Refuse		Health	
Garbage/Sewer		Dental	
Telephone		Disability	
Cellular Phone		Long Term	
Cable/Satellite/TiVo			
Internet			
Child Support			
Spousal Support			
		TOTAL FIXED EXPENSES	

INSTALLMENT EXPENSES

Loans/Credit Cards	Amount
TOTAL	

TOTAL EXPENSES

Total Fixed Expenses	
Total Installment Expenses	
Total Monthly Expenses from Below	
GRAND TOTAL EXPENSES	
Plus Amount Paid to Savings	

		RECREATION/ENTERTAINMENT/EDUCATION					FAMILY				GENERAL			
	vacation trips	entertain. DVD movies music parties	lottery sports hobbies lessons clubs	computer upgrades software supplies service	seminar workshop tuition supplies	newspaper books magazines software games/apps	elder care child care sitter tutor	infant exp. allowance school exp. toys arcades	pet vet supplies services sitter	gifts cards flowers	charitable contribut. church temple	work expense dues reimburse-ments	prof. services legal CPA investment	other (add explanation)
WEEK 1 — 1														
2														
3														
4														
5														
6														
7														
WEEK 2 — 8														
9														
10														
11														
12														
13														
14														
WEEK 3 — 15														
16														
17														
18														
19														
20														
21														
WEEK 4 — 22														
23														
24														
25														
26														
27														
28														
29														
30														
31														
T*														
B*														
D*														

* T = Total; B = Budget; D = Difference

Monthly Expense Record   139

MONTHLY EXPENSE RECORD

Balance Forward from Last Month:

Cash: _____ Checking: _____ Savings: _____

NET INCOME

			TOTAL
SALARY/COMMISSIONS			
	TOTAL INCOME		
OTHER			
	Subtotal Other Income		
	TOTAL NET INCOME		

SAVINGS

(Describe)	
TOTAL SAVINGS	

INVESTMENTS/RETIREMENT

TOTAL INVESTMENTS/RETIREMENT	

		FOOD		HOUSEHOLD				TRANSPORTATION			PERSONAL		HEALTH	
	groceries	cafeteria fast food dining out school lunches	tobacco alcohol snacks beverages water	cleaner mainten. house yard pool	appliances furniture furnishings supplies	postage copies ATM fees bank fees misc.	interest taxes	gas	auto mainten. wash license	taxi transit tolls/passes parking	clothing alterations dry clean. laundry shoe care	toiletries cosmetics hair nails massage	doctor dentist vision medicine vitamins	personal growth therapy
WEEK 1 — 1														
2														
3														
4														
5														
6														
7														
WEEK 2 — 8														
9														
10														
11														
12														
13														
14														
WEEK 3 — 15														
16														
17														
18														
19														
20														
21														
WEEK 4 — 22														
23														
24														
25														
26														
27														
28														
29														
30														
31														
T*														
B*														
D*														

* T = Total; B = Budget; D = Difference

MONTHLY EXPENSE RECORD

FIXED EXPENSES

Monthly	Amount	Monthly	Amount
Mortgage/Rent		Insurance:	
Assn. Fee		House/Apt	
Heating Oil/Gas		Auto	
Electricity		Life	
Water/Refuse		Health	
Garbage/Sewer		Dental	
Telephone		Disability	
Cellular Phone		Long Term	
Cable/Satellite/TiVo			
Internet			
Child Support			
Spousal Support			
		TOTAL FIXED EXPENSES	

INSTALLMENT EXPENSES

Loans/Credit Cards	Amount
TOTAL	

TOTAL EXPENSES

Total Fixed Expenses	
Total Installment Expenses	
Total Monthly Expenses from Below	
GRAND TOTAL EXPENSES	
Plus Amount Paid to Savings	

		RECREATION/ENTERTAINMENT/EDUCATION					FAMILY			GENERAL				
	vacation trips	entertain. DVD movies music parties	lottery sports hobbies lessons clubs	computer upgrades software supplies service	seminar workshop tuition supplies	newspaper books magazines software games/apps	elder care child care sitter tutor	infant exp. allowance school exp. toys arcades	pet vet supplies services sitter	gifts cards flowers	charitable contribut. church temple	work expense dues reimburse-ments	prof. services legal CPA investment	other (add explanation)
WEEK 1 1														
2														
3														
4														
5														
6														
7														
WEEK 2 8														
9														
10														
11														
12														
13														
14														
WEEK 3 15														
16														
17														
18														
19														
20														
21														
22														
23														
24														
WEEK 4 25														
26														
27														
28														
29														
30														
31														
T*														
B*														
D*														

* T = Total; B = Budget; D = Difference

MONTHLY EXPENSE RECORD

Balance Forward from Last Month:

Cash: _____ Checking: _____ Savings: _____

NET INCOME

			TOTAL
SALARY/COMMISSIONS			
TOTAL INCOME			
OTHER			
Subtotal Other Income			
TOTAL NET INCOME			

SAVINGS

(Describe)	
TOTAL SAVINGS	

INVESTMENTS/RETIREMENT

TOTAL INVESTMENTS/RETIREMENT	

		FOOD		HOUSEHOLD					TRANSPORTATION		PERSONAL		HEALTH	
	groceries	cafeteria fast food dining out school lunches	tobacco alcohol snacks beverages water	cleaner mainten. house yard pool	appliances furniture furnishings supplies	postage copies ATM fees bank fees misc.	interest taxes		gas	auto mainten. wash license	taxi transit tolls/passes parking	clothing alterations dry clean. laundry shoe care	toiletries cosmetics hair nails massage	doctor dentist vision medicine vitamins	personal growth therapy
WEEK 1 — 1															
2															
3															
4															
5															
6															
7															
WEEK 2 — 8															
9															
10															
11															
12															
13															
14															
WEEK 3 — 15															
16															
17															
18															
19															
20															
21															
WEEK 4 — 22															
23															
24															
25															
26															
27															
28															
29															
30															
31															
T*															
B*															
D*															

* T = Total; B = Budget; D = Difference

MONTHLY EXPENSE RECORD

FIXED EXPENSES

Monthly	Amount	Monthly	Amount
Mortgage/Rent		Insurance:	
Assn. Fee		House/Apt	
Heating Oil/Gas		Auto	
Electricity		Life	
Water/Refuse		Health	
Garbage/Sewer		Dental	
Telephone		Disability	
Cellular Phone		Long Term	
Cable/Satellite/TiVo			
Internet			
Child Support			
Spousal Support			
		TOTAL FIXED EXPENSES	

INSTALLMENT EXPENSES

Loans/Credit Cards	Amount
TOTAL	

TOTAL EXPENSES

Total Fixed Expenses	
Total Installment Expenses	
Total Monthly Expenses from Below	
GRAND TOTAL EXPENSES	
Plus Amount Paid to Savings	

	RECREATION/ENTERTAINMENT/EDUCATION						FAMILY				GENERAL				
	vacation trips	entertain. DVD movies music parties	lottery sports hobbies lessons clubs	computer upgrades software supplies service	seminar workshop tuition supplies	newspaper books magazines software games/apps	elder care child care sitter tutor	infant exp. allowance school exp. toys arcades	pet vet supplies services sitter	gifts cards flowers	charitable contribut. church temple	work expense dues reimburse-ments	prof. services legal CPA investment	other (add explanation)
WEEK 1 1														
2														
3														
4														
5														
6														
7														
WEEK 2 8														
9														
10														
11														
12														
13														
14														
WEEK 3 15														
16														
17														
18														
19														
20														
21														
WEEK 4 22														
23														
24														
25														
26														
27														
28														
29														
30														
31														
T*														
B*														
D*														

* T = Total; B = Budget; D = Difference

MONTHLY EXPENSE RECORD

Balance Forward from Last Month:

Cash: _____ Checking: _____ Savings: _____

NET INCOME

			TOTAL
SALARY/COMMISSIONS			
	TOTAL INCOME		
OTHER			
	Subtotal Other Income		
	TOTAL NET INCOME		

SAVINGS

(Describe)	
TOTAL SAVINGS	

INVESTMENTS/RETIREMENT

TOTAL INVESTMENTS/RETIREMENT	

	FOOD			HOUSEHOLD				TRANSPORTATION			PERSONAL		HEALTH	
	groceries	cafeteria fast food dining out school lunches	tobacco alcohol snacks beverages water	cleaner mainten. house yard pool	appliances furniture furnishings supplies	postage copies ATM fees bank fees misc.	interest taxes	gas	auto mainten. wash license	taxi transit tolls/passes parking	clothing alterations dry clean. laundry shoe care	toiletries cosmetics hair nails massage	doctor dentist vision medicine vitamins	personal growth therapy
WEEK 1 1 2 3 4 5 6 7														
WEEK 2 8 9 10 11 12 13 14														
WEEK 3 15 16 17 18 19 20 21														
WEEK 4 22 23 24 25 26 27 28 29 30 31														
T*														
B*														
D*														

* T = Total; B = Budget; D = Difference

MONTHLY EXPENSE RECORD

FIXED EXPENSES

Monthly	Amount	Monthly	Amount
Mortgage/Rent		Insurance:	
Assn. Fee		House/Apt	
Heating Oil/Gas		Auto	
Electricity		Life	
Water/Refuse		Health	
Garbage/Sewer		Dental	
Telephone		Disability	
Cellular Phone		Long Term	
Cable/Satellite/TiVo			
Internet			
Child Support			
Spousal Support			
		TOTAL FIXED EXPENSES	

INSTALLMENT EXPENSES

Loans/Credit Cards	Amount
TOTAL	

TOTAL EXPENSES

Total Fixed Expenses	
Total Installment Expenses	
Total Monthly Expenses from Below	
GRAND TOTAL EXPENSES	
Plus Amount Paid to Savings	

	RECREATION/ENTERTAINMENT/EDUCATION						FAMILY			GENERAL				
	vacation trips	entertain. DVD movies music parties	lottery sports hobbies lessons clubs	computer upgrades software supplies service	seminar workshop tuition supplies	newspaper books magazines software games/apps	elder care child care sitter tutor	infant exp. allowance school exp. toys arcades	pet vet supplies services sitter	gifts cards flowers	charitable contribut. church temple	work expense dues reimburse- ments	prof. services legal CPA investment	other (add explanation)
1														
W 2														
E 3														
E 4														
K 5														
1 6														
7														
8														
W 9														
E 10														
E 11														
K 12														
2 13														
14														
15														
W 16														
E 17														
E 18														
K 19														
3 20														
21														
22														
23														
24														
W 25														
E 26														
K 27														
4 28														
29														
30														
31														
T*														
B*														
D*														

* T = Total; B = Budget; D = Difference

Monthly Expense Record   145

MONTHLY EXPENSE RECORD

Balance Forward from Last Month:

Cash: _____ Checking: _____ Savings: _____

NET INCOME

			TOTAL
SALARY/COMMISSIONS			
		TOTAL INCOME	
OTHER			
		Subtotal Other Income	
		TOTAL NET INCOME	

SAVINGS

(Describe)	
TOTAL SAVINGS	

INVESTMENTS/RETIREMENT

TOTAL INVESTMENTS/RETIREMENT	

	FOOD			HOUSEHOLD				TRANSPORTATION			PERSONAL		HEALTH	
	groceries	cafeteria fast food dining out school lunches	tobacco alcohol snacks beverages water	cleaner mainten. house yard pool	appliances furniture furnishings supplies	postage copies ATM fees bank fees misc.	interest taxes	gas	auto mainten. wash license	taxi transit tolls/passes parking	clothing alterations dry clean. laundry shoe care	toiletries cosmetics hair nails massage	doctor dentist vision medicine vitamins	personal growth therapy
WEEK 1 — 1														
2														
3														
4														
5														
6														
7														
WEEK 2 — 8														
9														
10														
11														
12														
13														
14														
WEEK 3 — 15														
16														
17														
18														
19														
20														
21														
WEEK 4 — 22														
23														
24														
25														
26														
27														
28														
29														
30														
31														
T*														
B*														
D*														

* T = Total; B = Budget; D = Difference

MONTHLY EXPENSE RECORD

FIXED EXPENSES

Monthly	Amount	Monthly	Amount
Mortgage/Rent		Insurance:	
Assn. Fee		House/Apt	
Heating Oil/Gas		Auto	
Electricity		Life	
Water/Refuse		Health	
Garbage/Sewer		Dental	
Telephone		Disability	
Cellular Phone		Long Term	
Cable/Satellite/TiVo			
Internet			
Child Support			
Spousal Support			
		TOTAL FIXED EXPENSES	

INSTALLMENT EXPENSES

Loans/Credit Cards	Amount
TOTAL	

TOTAL EXPENSES

Total Fixed Expenses	
Total Installment Expenses	
Total Monthly Expenses from Below	
GRAND TOTAL EXPENSES	
Plus Amount Paid to Savings	

RECREATION/ENTERTAINMENT/EDUCATION — FAMILY — GENERAL

	vacation trips	entertain. DVD movies music parties	lottery sports hobbies lessons clubs	computer upgrades software supplies service	seminar workshop tuition supplies	newspaper books magazines software games/apps	elder care child care sitter tutor	infant exp. allowance school exp. toys arcades	pet vet supplies services sitter	gifts cards flowers	charitable contribut. church temple	work expense dues reimburse-ments	prof. services legal CPA investment	other (add explanation)
WEEK 1 1														
2														
3														
4														
5														
6														
7														
WEEK 2 8														
9														
10														
11														
12														
13														
14														
WEEK 3 15														
16														
17														
18														
19														
20														
21														
WEEK 4 22														
23														
24														
25														
26														
27														
28														
29														
30														
31														
T*														
B*														
D*														

* T = Total; B = Budget; D = Difference

MONTHLY EXPENSE RECORD

Balance Forward from Last Month:
Cash: _____ Checking: _____ Savings: _____

NET INCOME

			TOTAL
SALARY/COMMISSIONS			
TOTAL INCOME			
OTHER			
Subtotal Other Income			
TOTAL NET INCOME			

SAVINGS

(Describe)	
TOTAL SAVINGS	

INVESTMENTS/RETIREMENT

TOTAL INVESTMENTS/RETIREMENT	

	FOOD			HOUSEHOLD					TRANSPORTATION			PERSONAL		HEALTH	
	groceries	cafeteria fast food dining out school lunches	tobacco alcohol snacks beverages water	cleaner mainten. house yard pool	appliances furniture furnishings supplies	postage copies ATM fees bank fees misc.	interest taxes		gas	auto mainten. wash license	taxi transit tolls/passes parking	clothing alterations dry clean. laundry shoe care	toiletries cosmetics hair nails massage	doctor dentist vision medicine vitamins	personal growth therapy
WEEK 1 — 1															
2															
3															
4															
5															
6															
7															
WEEK 2 — 8															
9															
10															
11															
12															
13															
14															
WEEK 3 — 15															
16															
17															
18															
19															
20															
21															
WEEK 4 — 22															
23															
24															
25															
26															
27															
28															
29															
30															
31															
T*															
B*															
D*															

* T = Total; B = Budget; D = Difference

MONTHLY EXPENSE RECORD

FIXED EXPENSES

Monthly	Amount	Monthly	Amount
Mortgage/Rent		Insurance:	
Assn. Fee		House/Apt	
Heating Oil/Gas		Auto	
Electricity		Life	
Water/Refuse		Health	
Garbage/Sewer		Dental	
Telephone		Disability	
Cellular Phone		Long Term	
Cable/Satellite/TiVo			
Internet			
Child Support			
Spousal Support			
		TOTAL FIXED EXPENSES	

INSTALLMENT EXPENSES

Loans/Credit Cards	Amount
TOTAL	

TOTAL EXPENSES

Total Fixed Expenses	
Total Installment Expenses	
Total Monthly Expenses from Below	
GRAND TOTAL EXPENSES	
Plus Amount Paid to Savings	

	RECREATION/ENTERTAINMENT/EDUCATION						FAMILY			GENERAL					
	vacation trips	entertain. DVD movies music parties	lottery sports hobbies lessons clubs	computer upgrades software supplies service	seminar workshop tuition supplies	newspaper books magazines software games/apps	elder care child care sitter tutor	infant exp. allowance school exp. toys arcades	pet vet supplies services sitter	gifts cards flowers	charitable contribut. church temple	work expense dues reimburse-ments	prof. services legal CPA investment	other (add explanation)
WEEK 1 — 1														
2														
3														
4														
5														
6														
7														
WEEK 2 — 8														
9														
10														
11														
12														
13														
14														
WEEK 3 — 15														
16														
17														
18														
19														
20														
21														
WEEK 4 — 22														
23														
24														
25														
26														
27														
28														
29														
30														
31														
T*														
B*														
D*														

* T = Total; B = Budget; D = Difference

MONTHLY EXPENSE RECORD

Balance Forward from Last Month:

Cash: _____ Checking: _____ Savings: _____

NET INCOME

			TOTAL
SALARY/COMMISSIONS			
TOTAL INCOME			
OTHER			
Subtotal Other Income			
TOTAL NET INCOME			

SAVINGS

(Describe)	
TOTAL SAVINGS	

INVESTMENTS/RETIREMENT

TOTAL INVESTMENTS/RETIREMENT	

	FOOD			HOUSEHOLD				TRANSPORTATION			PERSONAL		HEALTH	
	groceries	cafeteria fast food dining out school lunches	tobacco alcohol snacks beverages water	cleaner mainten. house yard pool	appliances furniture furnishings supplies	postage copies ATM fees bank fees misc.	interest taxes	gas	auto mainten. wash license	taxi transit tolls/passes parking	clothing alterations dry clean. laundry shoe care	toiletries cosmetics hair nails massage	doctor dentist vision medicine vitamins	personal growth therapy
WEEK 1 — 1														
2														
3														
4														
5														
6														
7														
WEEK 2 — 8														
9														
10														
11														
12														
13														
14														
WEEK 3 — 15														
16														
17														
18														
19														
20														
21														
WEEK 4 — 22														
23														
24														
25														
26														
27														
28														
29														
30														
31														
T*														
B*														
D*														

* T = Total; B = Budget; D = Difference

MONTHLY EXPENSE RECORD

FIXED EXPENSES

Monthly	Amount	Monthly	Amount
Mortgage/Rent		Insurance:	
Assn. Fee		House/Apt	
Heating Oil/Gas		Auto	
Electricity		Life	
Water/Refuse		Health	
Garbage/Sewer		Dental	
Telephone		Disability	
Cellular Phone		Long Term	
Cable/Satellite/TiVo			
Internet			
Child Support			
Spousal Support			
		TOTAL FIXED EXPENSES	

INSTALLMENT EXPENSES

Loans/Credit Cards	Amount
TOTAL	

TOTAL EXPENSES

Total Fixed Expenses	
Total Installment Expenses	
Total Monthly Expenses from Below	
GRAND TOTAL EXPENSES	
Plus Amount Paid to Savings	

	RECREATION/ENTERTAINMENT/EDUCATION						FAMILY			GENERAL					
	vacation trips	entertain. DVD movies music parties	lottery sports hobbies lessons clubs	computer upgrades software supplies service	seminar workshop tuition supplies	newspaper books magazines software games/apps	elder care child care sitter tutor	infant exp. allowance school exp. toys arcades	pet vet supplies services sitter	gifts cards flowers	charitable contribut. church temple	work expense dues reimburse-ments	prof. services legal CPA investment	other (add explanation)
WEEK 1 1														
2														
3														
4														
5														
6														
7														
WEEK 2 8														
9														
10														
11														
12														
13														
14														
WEEK 3 15														
16														
17														
18														
19														
20														
21														
WEEK 4 22														
23														
24														
25														
26														
27														
28														
29														
30														
31														
T*														
B*														
D*														

* T = Total; B = Budget; D = Difference

Summary-for-the-Year Record/ End-of-the-Year Tax Information

The totals you have at the end of each month on the **Monthly Expense Record** can be transferred to this **Summary-for-the-Year Record** so you will have a total picture and a way to compare monthly expenses for each category. Having this summary information is excellent for measuring your financial progress and setting your future goals.

On the bottom of page 154, you also have a place for capturing your savings information with the **Summary for Monthly Savings/Investments/ Retirement** section. If you're looking for a quick snapshot of how much you put aside each month, whether through payroll withholdings for a 401(k) or similar plan or direct deposit to an account at a financial institution, this section provides a simple form to gather that information. The **End- of-the-Year Tax Information** worksheet on the bottom of page 155 offers a place to record your pay stub deduction information, such as your taxes, FICA, 401(k), 403(b), and other deductions. Again, this is a simple form for gathering that information in one place, provided this is how you like to organize information.

SUMMARY-FOR-THE-YEAR RECORD

		JAN.	FEB.	MAR.	APR.	MAY	JUNE	JULY	AUG.	SEPT.	OCT.	NOV.	DEC.	Total	Mo. Avg.
Net Income	Salary/ Commission														
	Other														
Food	Groceries														
	School Lunches, Dine Out, Fast Food														
	Snacks, Beverages, Alcohol, Tobacco														
Household	Supplies, Cleaners, Maintenance, House, Yard, Pool														
	Appliances, Furniture, Furnishings, Supplies														
	Postage, ATM Fees, Bank Charges, Misc.														
	Interest, Taxes														
Transportation	Gas														
	Automobile Maintenance, Wash, License														
	Transit, Tolls, Taxi, Parking														
Personal	Clothing, Alterations, Dry Cleaning, Laundry, Shoe Care														
	Cosmetics, Hair, Nails, Massage, Toiletries														
Health	Doctor, Dentist, Vision, Medicine, Vitamins														
	Personal Growth Therapy														
Recreation	Vacation, Trips														
	Entertain., DVD, Movies, Music, Parties														
	Sports, Hobbies, Lessons, Clubs, Lottery														
	Computer, Upgrades, Software, Supplies, Service														

SUMMARY FOR MONTHLY SAVINGS/INVESTMENTS/RETIREMENT

	JAN.	FEB.	MAR.	APR.	MAY	JUNE	JULY	AUG.	SEPT.	OCT.	NOV.	DEC.	Total
Savings													
Investments													
Retirement													
Total													

		JAN.	FEB.	MAR.	APR.	MAY	JUNE	JULY	AUG.	SEPT.	OCT.	NOV.	DEC.	Total	Mo. Avg.
Education	Tuition, Supplies, Workshops, Seminars														
Education	Books, Magazines, Software, Newspaper, Games														
Family	Elder Care, Child Care, Sitter, Tutor														
Family	Allowance, Toys, Infant Exp., School Exp., Arcades														
Family	Pet, Vet, Supplies, Services														
General	Gifts, Cards, Flowers														
General	Charitable Contribut., Church, Temple														
General	Work Expense, Dues														
General	Prof. Serv., Legal, CPA, Investment														
General	Other														
Home	Mortgage, Rent, Assn. Fees														
Utilities	Gas, Electric														
Utilities	Water, Garbage														
Utilities	Phone, Cable, ISP														
Support	Child, Spousal, Club														
Insur.	Home, Auto, Life, Health, Disability, Storage														
Install.	Loans, Credit Cards														
Total	Monthly Expenses														

END-OF-THE-YEAR TAX INFORMATION

	JAN.	FEB.	MAR.	APR.	MAY	JUNE	JULY	AUG.	SEPT.	OCT.	NOV.	DEC.	Total
Federal													
State													
FICA													
Other Deductions													
Total													

Part Three

This collection of worksheets, for keeping records and recording expenses, will help you keep your financial records organized. Look through each of these forms to see which worksheets apply to you and will be helpful for your particular household's financial situation.

Medical Expense Record

Flexible Spending Account Record

Tax-Deductible Expense Record

Miscellaneous Expense Record

Investment/Savings Record

Savings Activity Record

Retirement Savings Record

Child Support Records

Subscription Record

Online and Mail Order Purchase Record

Medical Expense Record

If you need to keep additional records on medical expenses, use these worksheets. The first page, "Doctor, Dentist, and Hospital Visits," can be used for recording all visits, including nontraditional health care. Include the costs here whether they are full pay, co-pay, or are going to be reimbursed by insurance. If you have a lot of prescriptions, lab tests, and other related medical expenses (like glasses, crutches, rental medical equipment), then use the second page, "Medical Expenses, Prescriptions, and Other" to keep those expense records separate.

For those households with extensive medical expenses, you may want to make extra copies of these forms ahead of time. Some people use separate sheets for each family member. Again, these worksheets are a guideline so adjust them to work for your medical recordkeeping needs.

A space is provided for mileage, which at this writing is tax-deductible. The columns for "Date Submitted" and "Insurance Reimbursements" are provided for those households paying the medical bills first before submitting claims or paying the differences not covered by insurance and wanting to keep this information separate.

During tax time, this information will save you hours of preparation time.

MEDICAL EXPENSE RECORD

DOCTOR, DENTIST, AND HOSPITAL VISITS

Date	Mileage	To Whom Paid	Amount	Date Submitted	Insurance Reimbursements Amount/Date Paid
		Total			
		Total Amount Paid			
		Total Reimbursed			
		Total Medical Cost			

MEDICAL EXPENSE RECORD

Date	Mileage	To Whom Paid	Amount	Date Submitted	Insurance Reimbursements Amount/Date Paid
Total					
Total Amount Paid					
Total Reimbursed					
Total Medical Cost					

Flexible Spending Account Record

More companies are offering flexible spending accounts (FSAs), which allow their employees to save pretax dollars for certain health care and dependent day care expenses. Your employer will explain how the program works, the maximum contribution amounts, and qualifying expenses, and will give you estimating worksheets so you can determine how much money to plan to contribute to your FSA.

These accounts can be very valuable if you use them to their fullest advantage and diligently keep your records and receipts. The tricky part is carefully balancing what you believe will be all the estimated expenses against the actual total expenses at the end of the year. Because this is a "use it or lose it" program, you face the risk of forfeiting any unused money at the end of the year. Therefore, the purpose of this **Flexible Spending Account Record** is to provide a form for all your records so that you don't miss any qualifying expenses. Make additional copies ahead of time if you anticipate extensive activity and records. Be sure to have a folder where you keep all the matching receipts. All of this information will be required at the end of the year.

FLEXIBLE SPENDING ACCOUNT RECORD

Each account must be separate. Money in one account cannot be used for the other account.

Health Care Expenses (Medical, Dental, Vision Deductibles, Co-pays, Coinsurance, Prescription Co-pays, Other)
Dependent Care Expenses (Child/Elder Care, Eligible School & Summer Programs, Kindergarten/Nursery School Expenses)

Date	Description of Expense	Cost	Date Claim Submitted	Reimbursed	Notes

Tax-Deductible Expense Record

After you record your expenses on the **Monthly Expense Record** worksheets, take a moment to jot down deductible expenses on the **Tax-Deductible Expense Record** so you have all your deductible expenses recorded in one place. When you prepare next year's tax return, itemizing deductions will be a very quick and efficient process.

Each year, tax deductions may vary. This worksheet is designed to be a convenient record of all deductions applying to your circumstances and the current tax laws. Include categories such as *education, professional or union dues, child care, alimony, casualty losses, etc.* If you have regular or multiple deductions in *one category,* the **Multiple Tax-Deductible Expense Record** on page 168 may be more convenient for recording those amounts.

Consult your tax professional regarding any changes in tax law for these or any other tax-related records.

> *"The IRS audited my records and said they were so good it was no problem and they accepted all of it. My insurance company also accepted my records without having receipts. I'm 68 years old and have used this book for ten years, and I'm buying ten more for the next ten years."*

Home Business

More and more households seem to be starting up small home businesses, online businesses, or getting into different kinds of network marketing to generate extra income. The next step is a basic system for recording business income and expenses to be better prepared for taxes. *The Budget Kit* does offer the same basic concepts that one would use for personal budgeting as well as budgeting for a small business; however, I prefer to recommend some dedicated business resources.

The following two resources are simple and straightforward, giving you all the basic tools you need for organizing your home business and tax records:

1. Tax Minimi$er™—For Small and Home-Based Businesses and Self-Employed Entrepreneurs, The Daily Plan-It, LLC, *www.taxminimiser.com*
2. *It's How Much You Keep That Counts! Not How Much You Make. The ONLY 'Plain English' Step-by-Step Guide to Home-Business Tax Breaks Authorized by Congress,* Ronald R. Mueller, MBA, PhD, *www.homebusinesstaxsavings.com*

TAX-DEDUCTIBLE EXPENSE RECORD

YEAR 20____

Date	Description (Donation/Payment To)	Check Number	Amount/Value: Taxes/Interest	Charitable Contribution	_____	_____
	Total					

MULTIPLE TAX-DEDUCTIBLE EXPENSE RECORD

YEAR 20____

CATEGORY: _____

Date	Description	Amount
	Total	

CATEGORY: _____

Date	Description	Amount
	Total	

MULTIPLE TAX-DEDUCTIBLE EXPENSE RECORD

YEAR 20____

CATEGORY: _____

Date	Description	Amount
Total		

CATEGORY: _____

Date	Description	Amount
Total		

Miscellaneous Expense Record

A variety of additional generic worksheets are provided for other records, such as major household purchases, home improvement projects, car expenses, and college costs. You have the option of either recording a variety of expenses as they occur or using a dedicated form for tracking specific category expenses by the month. Use any of these or the other variety of worksheets in this workbook to best fit your particular needs.

RECORD OF _____   MISCELLANEOUS EXPENSE RECORD YEAR 20____

	JAN.	FEB.	MAR.	APR.	MAY	JUNE	JULY	AUG.	SEPT.	OCT.	NOV.	DEC.	TOTAL
Total													

MISCELLANEOUS EXPENSE RECORD

YEAR 20____

Date	To Whom Paid/Service	Amount
	Total	

Date	To Whom Paid/Service	Amount
	Total	

MISCELLANEOUS EXPENSE RECORD

Date	To Whom Paid/Service	Amount
	Total	

Date	To Whom Paid/Service	Amount
	Total	

Investment/Savings Record

Your Investment Picture

If you followed the suggestions and guidelines in this workbook, you probably already have or soon will have some basic savings and investments.

Whether you have money in company savings plans, inherited some stocks and bonds, invested in mutual funds, changed your savings to certificates of deposit (CDs) or money markets, or opened a Roth or traditional individual retirement account (IRA), it is important to keep all your records in one place and know what you have. These records are extremely useful for preparing income tax, completing financial statements, and helping your heirs in the event of an unexpected death.

As with personal finances, if you don't pay attention to your investments or keep careful records of them, you may easily forget what you have or where your investments are held. Soon it may be hard to remember just exactly where you put those IRAs or CDs that you purchased sometime in 1999 or 2008. What rates are they getting? What are the maturity dates?

Or maybe through your parents or a divorce, you acquired some stocks that are just "sitting" in an account, and you really don't know what you have. With today's fast-paced lifestyle, it is easy to leave the responsibility of knowing what you own to someone else—a banker, a broker, or an accountant—but by doing so, you sacrifice an understanding and awareness of your total financial picture.

The **Investment/Savings Record** on pages 178–179 provides a place for recording key information about your various investments. The space on the right on page 179 allows for a periodic follow-up of your current yield. The headings are used as a guideline. If necessary, change them to make them appropriate for your investments.

If you anticipate frequent changes, you could record general information at the beginning of the year here and use the other worksheets in this section of the workbook to record your investment and savings activity. You can modify the **Savings Activity Record, Retirement Savings Record**, or **Miscellaneous Expense Record** to fit your needs. The important point is to be sure that you have recorded all the information for each of your investments and have it all in one convenient place.

Reserve Funds

Use this section of the **Investment/Savings Record** to record information about your liquid-asset accounts (money you have available for immediate use without withdrawal penalties). These include investments in money market accounts or savings in your bank and/or credit union.

If you have ongoing monthly savings activity, you can use the **Savings Activity Record** on page 180 to record your month-to-month transactions. On that page, you can list your savings for upcoming taxes or insurance (reserve account), unexpected car or home repairs (emergency account), or vacation and Christmas/holiday savings (goal account).

Some people like to put all these different savings in one account and then use this worksheet for keeping records of the separate activity.

Retirement

Your monthly retirement savings activity can be recorded on the **Retirement Savings Record** on page 181 in this section. These programs range from savings funded and/or established by your employer, to personal IRAs, Keoghs, tax-sheltered annuities (TSAs), company pensions, and other tax-sheltered investments.

A wide variety of employee-retirement programs are offered through schools, hospitals, government, and private firms. It is easy to forget or ignore these funds, for they often are only shown as paycheck deductions. Pay attention to and gather up the necessary information as outlined in this section so you are familiar with your current and past retirement programs.

Short- and Long-Term Holdings

Record your investments held for short or extended periods on the **Investment/Savings Record**. Some of these investments, such as CDs, T-bills, bonds, etc., will have fixed rates or time periods, and this information should be noted on the worksheet. With other securities (stocks, mutual funds, and options), prices can change daily. Because there is limited space for all the variable information, use this worksheet for beginning- and end-of-the-year summaries.

If you frequently buy and sell, and actively get involved with your investments, you probably already have an investment portfolio online and/or with your broker with all the necessary information. On the other hand, if you do not do much with your investments, especially securities, *the information on this worksheet will be extremely helpful for tax, loan, or net worth purposes.*

Other Investments

Your investments, such as real estate (other than personal residence), collectibles, trusts, or limited or general partnerships, would also be recorded on this **Investment/Savings Record**. If the majority of those other investments are quite extensive, however, you probably have them recorded through another system. If so, indicate where you have those records. The same is true for any of your other investments listed on this worksheet. Be sure your spouse and/or family know where to locate all this information and any necessary passwords and any lockbox, safe, or keys.

Maintaining Control of Your Finances

As you gather your investment information, you may find you need to develop your own follow-up system for those long-range investments with maturity dates. Start a file and keep a copy of these worksheets for each year. Highlight the maturity dates so you have a quick reference.

While reviewing your investments, take time to monitor the returns and determine how well your investments are performing.

These worksheets, along with the others you have used in this workbook, will help you to record all your financial information in one place, thus staying organized and aware of your finances.

THE ONLINE/ELECTRONIC CONNECTION TO *THE BUDGET KIT*

Online banking and investing now available through your bank, brokerage firm, or other services make it possible to keep detailed records of all your savings and investments securely online. Take advantage of all the comprehensive financial websites for doing your research and monitoring your investments.

The **Investment/Savings Record** can be used as your basic paper backup information center for your spouse or family when they need to locate your investment information. Keep a summary list of the investments and the URL addresses for the websites you are using. Be sure to include any other contact information, user name, or password that would also be helpful.

Note: If you decide to fully utilize the investment and savings records in this section, you may be considering the idea of adding your user name and password information to be thoroughly organized. This is certainly one handy way to manually centralize all this security information. However, in today's heightened identity theft consciousness, it is important to be very careful about where we keep sensitive information. If you do decide to enter any security information in this workbook, I would recommend you tear out the pages and save them in another location for safe keeping.

INVESTMENT/SAVINGS RECORD

RESERVE FUNDS (Checking, Savings, Money Market, etc.)

Name of Institution	Type	Account Number	Date Opened	Amount Invested	Interest Rate	Owned By (husband, wife, joint)

RETIREMENT ACCOUNTS (IRA, Roth, 401(k), 403(b), SEP, Keogh, etc.)

Where Held	Type and Name	Account Number	Purchase Date	Amount Invested	Allocation

SHORT- AND LONG-TERM HOLDINGS (Mutual Funds, Stocks, Bonds, etc.)

Where Held	Type and Name	Certificate/ Account Number	Purchase Date	Amount Invested	Number of Shares	Unit Price	Dividend/ Interest Rate

OTHER (Real Estate, Collectibles, etc.)

Location/Name	Date Purchased	Cost	Monthly/Yearly Income	Location of Records

INVESTMENT/SAVINGS RECORD

Contact Name/Telephone	Location of Records	Follow-Up Information (date, balance, current yield)

RETIREMENT ACCOUNTS

Owned By (husband, wife, joint)	Contact Name/ Telephone	Location of Records	Date Sold	Distribution Amount	Additional Notes (rollover information)

SHORT- AND LONG-TERM HOLDINGS

Date/Amount Dividend Paid	Maturity Date	Owned By (husband, wife, joint)	Contact Name/ Telephone	Location of Records	Date Sold	Number of Shares Sold	Net Proceeds	Gain/ Loss

OTHER

Owned By (husband, wife, joint)	Date Sold	Proceeds	Gain/Loss	Additional Notes

SAVINGS ACTIVITY RECORD

EMERGENCY

Institution: _____   Account Number: _____

	JAN.	FEB.	MAR.	APR.	MAY	JUNE	JULY	AUG.	SEPT.	OCT.	NOV.	DEC.
Deposits												
Withdrawals												
Interest Earned												
Balance												

RESERVE

Institution: _____   Account Number: _____

	JAN.	FEB.	MAR.	APR.	MAY	JUNE	JULY	AUG.	SEPT.	OCT.	NOV.	DEC.
Deposits												
Withdrawals												
Interest Earned												
Balance												

GOALS/CHRISTMAS AND HOLIDAY

Institution: _____   Account Number: _____

	JAN.	FEB.	MAR.	APR.	MAY	JUNE	JULY	AUG.	SEPT.	OCT.	NOV.	DEC.
Deposits												
Withdrawals												
Interest Earned												
Balance												

OTHER

Institution: _____   Account Number: _____

	JAN.	FEB.	MAR.	APR.	MAY	JUNE	JULY	AUG.	SEPT.	OCT.	NOV.	DEC.
Deposits												
Withdrawals												
Interest Earned												
Balance												

RETIREMENT SAVINGS RECORD

NAME

Date	Program (IRA, 401(k), etc.): _____ _____ _____			Date	Program (IRA, 401(k), etc.): _____ _____ _____		
Total				**Total**			

NAME

Date	Program (IRA, 401(k), etc.): _____ _____ _____			Date	Program (IRA, 401(k), etc.): _____ _____ _____		
Total				**Total**			

Child Support Records

"Earlier this year I needed a personal loan. I couldn't have qualified if I had no proof of child support. The record in this workbook was sufficient information for the bank's approval."

Keeping Records

After a divorce, it is so easy for depression, anger, fear, and loneliness to interfere with practical thoughts and actions.

During this time, credit problems often crop up. This is not because you are incapable of managing your money, but often because you are suddenly overwhelmed with handling all the aspects of family life and household maintenance. Due dates, bills, and paperwork may just seem to get away from you.

Keeping proper records of child support payments, children's expenses, and pertinent custody information is extremely important. However, because of the demands of trying to meet the physical and emotional needs of your children and yourself, these records are often neglected or are never established.

The following worksheets were designed to help remove some of the burden of keeping important records. *The worksheets provide guidelines to help you remember what records you should keep and provide you with a tool for having all your necessary information and records in one place.* By organizing and controlling this aspect of your life, you will be better equipped to move on to other pressing issues that you face every day.

If you are the noncustodial parent making the child support payments, recording the information called for can be just as important for you. If you must prove what amount and when a support payment was actually made, received, and cashed or must prove other significant information for tax or legal purposes, you will have the necessary records.

Utilize and modify the worksheets in this book so that you can record information that is unique to your needs. For example, you may want to use the Medical and Dental Expense section of this workbook for keeping detailed records of who paid a medical expense, the insurance deductible, or the difference not paid by insurance.

When using these worksheets, be aware that the state and federal laws and regulations vary. *The worksheets and text are not a substitute for legal advice from your local attorney. Consult with your attorney for any questions in this section.*

Child Support Payment Record

This record on page 186 is critical when you need help from your local enforcement agency because of late, short, or missing payments. The "Amount Due" ① column is for the monthly child support payment as ordered. Enter the amount received under the month it was *due*. If no payment was received that month, note that under "Amount Received." ② Because these payments may vary from once a week, or once a month, to sporadically for the year, you will have to modify this column to fit your needs.

Record the other related child support obligations as ordered by the divorce decree, such as medical insurance premium, unreimbursed medical expense, tuition, dues, etc. ③ Also keep records of conversations concerning finances with your case workers, ex-spouse, and others. Keep a copy of your decree, stating the terms, payment, custody, visitation, conditions of support, and your record of conversations in a convenient file.

Note under "Additional Information" ④ if an item was substituted in lieu of a child support payment. Be sure to check with your attorney if this is an *acceptable form of child support*. If you do not wish to accept an item in lieu of a payment, ask your attorney if written notice should be given. If so, be sure to keep a copy.

When recording the institution, number, and date of the check or money order, ⑤ use the symbols shown to indicate how the payment was made. If possible, keep a copy of all checks, money orders, and envelopes, especially if there is a regular problem with support being on time. These copies will be helpful if a court or social agency ever needs to review your records in the event that there is an excessive lag between the date of the check and the date it was sent or if payment was stopped on a check or money order you received. Be sure to note if you are unable to make a copy of the checks, money orders, or envelopes.

You will find that this worksheet will contain some of your most important records. Stay with it.

The Cost of Raising Children

If you need or want to analyze the cost of raising your children, to show the use of support provided or to demonstrate the need for increased support, use the **Monthly Expense Record** section in Part Two.

Enter all your children's daily expenses along with all your other expenses on the **Monthly Expense Record** pages. Modify the headings to fit your individual needs. Use a highlighter, colored pencil, or check mark to show which expenses are the children's. If you are using the Excel **Monthly Expense Record** worksheet, there are many ways to highlight and separate expenses, whether by highlighting cells with different colors or by adding comment boxes. Total the children's expenses in the columns that apply and record the total at the bottom of the page below the family total. If you have a question about allocating expenses shared by you and your children, ask your local attorney.

Another method used by some families for keeping accurate records is a separate checking account and/or a credit card used strictly for children's expenses. Use the method that works best for you.

If you save all your receipts in envelopes labeled for the different categories, you can file these in your filing system.

Child Support Enforcement and Child Visitation Records

In 1984, Congress passed the Child Support Enforcement Amendments of 1984 that strengthen the child support enforcement laws throughout the country. The child support information you record on pages 186–187 will be invaluable if you ever need the services of a Child Support Enforcement Bureau in your state to help you collect past-due child support.

If you would like more information about Child Support Enforcement, there is a publication called "Handbook on Child Support Enforcement" available online at *www.acf.hhs.gov/programs/cse/pubs/2005/handbook_on_cse.pdf*. The U.S. Department of Health and Human Services features the Office of Child Support Enforcement website *www.acf.hhs.gov/programs/cse* where you'll find a wealth of additional information.

You can also order the free publication by phone or mail, but you will need to add a $2 service charge. To contact the Federal Citizen Information Center (FCIC), call 888-878-3256 and ask for publication number 505P. Or write to FCIC-07B, P.O. Box 100, Pueblo, CO 81002. Make the check to "Superintendent of Documents." This agency also has a website at *www.pueblo.gsa.gov*. Click on the "Family" section for more publications. While on the website, take a look at their "Money" section for some great publications.

On page 187, there is a basic **Child Visitation Record** form provided to give you a way to record the specific dates of visitation each month. There definitely will be times when this information will be requested, and this can serve as your running documentation.

Reduced Anxiety

These worksheets cannot take away the pain. They can, however, help reduce some of the anxiety associated with the aftermath of a divorce. As you start taking charge of your situation and gain new knowledge, you will regain self-confidence and self-esteem in the process.

Best of luck to you!

CHILD SUPPORT PAYMENT RECORD

Balance Due (from previous year) $ _____

Month	① Amount Due	② Amount Received	Amount Past Due	⑤ Number on: ×–$ Order ✓–Check $–Cash	Date on: ×–$ Order ✓–Check $–Cash	Date Payment Received	⑤ Institution and Account Number	③ Other Expenses*	④ Additional Information/ Action Taken (check status, gifts, etc.)
JAN.									
FEB.									
MAR.									
APR.									
MAY									
JUNE									
JULY									
AUG.									
SEPT.									
OCT.									
NOV.									
DEC.									
Total									

*Stipulated by decree

NOTES:

CHILD SUPPORT ENFORCEMENT RECORD

Noncustodial Parent

Full Name

_____

Last Known Address(es)

_____

_____

_____

Address Dates _____

Home Telephone

_____

Social Security Number

_____

Birth Date/Place _____

_____

Height _____ Weight _____

Occupation

_____

Last Known Employer(s)

_____

Address

_____

_____

_____

Address Dates _____

Work Telephone

_____

_____

Child Support Enforcement Office

Address

_____

_____

_____

Telephone Number

_____

Case Worker's Name/Telephone

_____

_____

Case Number

_____

Court Order Number

_____

Note: Get a Birth Registration Card from your Vital Statistics Office. This will have all your children's information printed on it so you will have the information handy.

CHILD VISITATION RECORD

DATES OF VISITATION

JAN.	FEB.	MAR.	APR.	MAY	JUNE	JULY	AUG.	SEPT.	OCT.	NOV.	DEC.

Subscription Record

If you ever waited three months to receive your subscription or learned that your magazine gift took that long before it was ever received, you will appreciate having all this information at your fingertips.

Having this record is an easy way to organize all your subscription amounts and dates due in one central place. It will also help prevent any double payments. You can then transfer this information to the **Yearly Budget Worksheet** in Part Two where all your nonmonthly expenses are listed on one convenient page.

SUBSCRIPTION RECORD

Publication:					
Subscription Through: Agency Address					
Telephone					
Date Ordered					
Amount Paid					
Check # or Credit Card Used					
Length (1, 2, 3 yrs.)					
Expiration Date					
Arrival Date					
Gift For:					
Other					

Publication:					
Subscription Through: Agency Address					
Telephone					
Date Ordered					
Amount Paid					
Check # or Credit Card Used					
Length (1, 2, 3 yrs.)					
Expiration Date					
Arrival Date					
Gift For:					
Other					

Online and Mail Order Purchase Record

Mail Order, Internet, and TV Shopping

There are obvious advantages to shopping by mail or online, including convenience, saving time, and discount savings. However, how many times have you ordered something by mail, telephone, or Internet expecting it to arrive, and it never did? Or how about TV infomercials and shopping channels hawking the latest beauty, weight loss, or entertainment products offered with a 30-day money-back guarantee? Chances are you have had your share of mail order frustrations, undelivered orders, or unsatisfactory products. You may also have had more items than you care to admit continue to show up each month and be charged to your credit card, because you failed to call and cancel the program after the original product arrived. If so, now you probably recognize the value of keeping clearer records for follow-up and cancellation purposes.

How to Keep Records

If orders do not arrive as scheduled and follow-up action is necessary, this **Online and Mail Order Purchase Record** will be a valuable time and money saver for you.

Use this form for all items ordered even if they are free. Keeping track of rebates will also work on this form. Log the necessary information related to any purchases made by mail, telephone, or online. When you happen to remember an item you ordered some time ago and realize it still has not arrived, you can check these records, see when you ordered the item, then follow up by the appropriate method.

In some cases, it may be easier to cut out the ad with all the information given and tape it to this page or in the back of this workbook. Then fill in only the "Total Sent" and "How Paid" sections. If you order a list of items from one catalog, make a copy of the order form and save it. On this page, make a note of the order, the catalog date, and how and when you paid for it. The same is true for online orders. Print out a copy of the order, including the confirmation number, and save that copy with your records or in the back of this workbook.

When placing a telephone order or following up on an order, be especially careful to record all the information on this worksheet, including the name of the person you spoke to or who took your order. Also, ask immediately for the number to call if you want to cancel, and note it on this form to save you future headaches.

Safety Online

Shop with the companies you know. If you want to learn more about an unfamiliar company before ordering, ask them to send you information or a catalog. Be sure to find out the company's policies on refunds and returns before placing any order.

Find out if your browser is secure before purchasing anything online. Note if there is a lock icon on the screen. Some browsers use a closed lock icon to indicate a secure session. A secure session is extremely important when you provide personal information such as credit card number, name, address, and phone number over the Internet.

Remember, if you pay with a credit card and have problems with your order, you have the advantage of having the right to dispute your charges. Your creditor will investigate the circumstances while you temporarily withhold payment. The complaint and situation will need to be explained and submitted in writing. Having the records on this page will make that process easier for you.

Be careful with your password. Never give it to anyone. Use a password you can readily remember but which is not as obvious as your birthday, telephone number, license, or Social Security number.

Enjoy these conveniences that now exist, but do so with appropriate caution.

Federal Trade Commission (FTC) Mail Order Rule

The Federal Trade Commission's (FTC) Mail or Telephone Order Merchandising Rule requires companies to ship an order within the time period mentioned in their advertisements. If no time period is given, the company is required to ship an order within 30 days of receipt of your payment. The company must notify you if it cannot make the shipment within 30 days and send you an option notice of either consenting to a delay or canceling the order for a refund.

For more information on e-commerce and the Internet, or consumer information in general, visit *www.ftc.gov/bcp/consumer.shtm*. You will find a wealth of valuable consumer information.

ONLINE AND MAIL ORDER PURCHASE RECORD

Date Ordered					

Item(s) Ordered
  Title
  Description
  Number
  Quantity
  Color					

Source (Internet, magazine, TV, catalog)					
Confirmation Number					

Company Name
  Telephone Number
  Address
  Account No.					

Price					
Total Sent					
How Paid*					
Date Received					
30-Day Return Date					
Cancellation Phone Number					
Follow-Up Notes (date called/wrote, contact person, action taken)					

*Credit card, check number, money order, COD, online bill pay

Date Ordered					

Item(s) Ordered
  Title
  Description
  Number
  Quantity
  Color					

Source (Internet, magazine, TV, catalog)					
Confirmation Number					

Company Name
  Telephone Number
  Address
  Account No.					

Price					
Total Sent					
How Paid*					
Date Received					
30-Day Return Date					
Cancellation Phone Number					
Follow-Up Notes (date called/wrote, contact person, action taken)					

*Credit card, check number, money order, COD, online bill pay

ONLINE AND MAIL ORDER PURCHASE RECORD

Date Ordered					
Item(s) Ordered 　Title 　Description 　Number 　Quantity 　Color					
Source (Internet, magazine, TV, catalog)					
Confirmation Number					
Company Name 　Telephone Number 　Address 　Account No.					
Price					
Total Sent					
How Paid*					
Date Received					
30-Day Return Date					
Cancellation Phone Number					
Follow-Up Notes (date called/wrote, contact person, action taken)					

*Credit card, check number, money order, COD, online bill pay

Date Ordered					
Item(s) Ordered 　Title 　Description 　Number 　Quantity 　Color					
Source (Internet, magazine, TV, catalog)					
Confirmation Number					
Company Name 　Telephone Number 　Address 　Account No.					
Price					
Total Sent					
How Paid*					
Date Received					
30-Day Return Date					
Cancellation Phone Number					
Follow-Up Notes (date called/wrote, contact person, action taken)					

*Credit card, check number, money order, COD, online bill pay

Acknowledgments

My special thanks go to the following people who helped with the development of this new and revised version of *The Budget Kit: The Common Cents Money Management Workbook*, along with the new digital formats, or gave their support and encouragement as this book metamorphosed through its *Common Cents* years into the workbook you now hold:

- Shannon Berning, Acquisitions Editor, who encouraged and supported this revision and the talented members of the Kaplan team—Amy Novak, Product Manager, Kate Lopaze, Development Editor, and Fred Urfer, Production Editor—who created this fresh new format.

- All my many wonderful readers and clients around the world who have used this workbook year after year and have shared their stories, ideas, and suggestions. Your shared insights have been used in the past editions and continue to be valuable once again in this latest edition.

- Rick and Peggy Harter, my long-standing Albuquerque friends, who mean the world to me. I will be forever grateful for their ongoing love, caring, and incredibly generous support. They helped create a seamless transition back to New Mexico. Who would have guessed, so many years ago when these two young college grads moved next door to me, how connected our lives would be in the future?

- Marcia and Gary Kons, the two most loving, supportive, encouraging, and wise friends anyone could be blessed to have. Their shared physical and emotional strength literally helped me move, on many levels, to the ideal place and situation to write many new editions.

- Carol Park, my professional colleague and friend, who continues to inspire me with her work, ideas, and strong determination.

- And again to my dear New Zealand friends Jessica, Misha, Inga, Ans, and Althea and my other beautiful Queststar sisters whose healing wisdom and love will always be a part of who I am and each new book I write.

Recommended Reading

The following books and other resources are included because of their total focus or special sections on *budgeting, credit, debt, spending, money attitudes,* and/or *recovery issues* or how money issues relate to couples, women, seniors, or 20 to 30 year olds. If you want more financial planning information, there are numerous excellent books with a full range and comprehensive coverage of all facets of personal finance available at your local book stores, library, or through the Web.

If managing money is new for you, these books offer a variety of ideas, approaches, and information to help you get started. The following books can provide complementary information as you do the practical hands-on part with *The Budget Kit: Common Cents Money Management Workbook.*

The 9 Steps to Financial Freedom: Practical and Spiritual Steps So You Can Stop Worrying, Suze Orman (Three Rivers Press, 2006).

The AARP Retirement Survival Guide: How to Make Smart Financial Decisions in Good Times and Bad, Julie Jason (Sterling, 2009).

Addicted to Shopping and Other Issues Women Have with Money, Karen O'Connor (Harvest House Publishers, 2005).

Ask and It Is Given: Learning to Manifest Your Desires, Esther and Jerry Hicks (Hay House, Inc, 2005).

Become Totally Debt-Free in Five Years or Less, Gwendolyn D. Gabriel, et al. (Brown Bag Press, 2000).

Born to Spend, Gloria Arenson (Brockart Books, 2003).

Bounce Back from Bankruptcy, 4th ed., Paula Langguth Ryan (Pellingham Casper Communications, 2007)

The Complete Idiot's Guide to Personal Finance in Your 20s and 30s, Sarah Young Fisher, Susan Shelly, and Grace W. Weinstein (Alpha Books, 2009).

Conscious Spending for Couples: Seven Skills for Financial Harmony, Deborah Knuckey (Wiley, John & Sons, Inc. 2002).

Consuming Passions: Help for Compulsive Shoppers, Ellen Mohr Catalano (New Harbinger Publications, 1993).

Credit Repair, Robin Leonard, JD, and John Lamb, attorney (Nolo, 2009).

The Credit Repair Handbook: Everything You Need to Know to Maintain, Rebuild, and Protect Your Credit, John Ventura (Kaplan Publishing, 2007).

Currency of Hope, Debtors Anonymous General Service Board of Trustees, Inc. (1999).

Deal with Your Debt: The Right Way to Manage Your Bills and Pay Off What You Owe, Liz Pulliam Weston (Prentice Hall, 2005).

Debt Cure$ "They" Don't Want You to Know About, Kevin Trudeau (Equity Press, 2008).

Debt-Free Forever: Take Control of Your Money and Your Life, Gail Vaz-Oxlade (The Experiment, 2010).

Debt-Proof Living: The Complete Guide to Living Financially Free, Mary Hunt (DPL Press, Inc., 2006).

"Don't Worry About a Thing Dear": Why Women Need Financial Intimacy, Helga Hayes (PrimeLife Publishing, 2006).

The Energy of Money: A Spiritual Guide to Financial and Personal Fulfillment, Maria Nemeth, PhD (Wellspring/Ballantine, 2000).

The Everything Budgeting Book, Tere Drenth (Adams Media Corporation, 2008).

The Everything Personal Finance in Your 20s and 30s: Erase Your Debt, Personalize Your Budget, and Plan Now to Secure Your Future, Debby Fowles (Adams Media, 2008).

The Everything Personal Finance in Your 40s and 50s Book: A Comprehensive Strategy to Ensure You Can Retire When You Want and Live Well, Jennifer and Bill Lane (Adams Media, 2008).

The Family Budget Blueprint: A Short Guide to Keep You "Out of the Red" with Your Family Finances, Martin Samson (CreateSpace, 2010).

The Family Financial Workbook: A Practical Guide to Budgeting, Larry Burkett (Moody Publishers, 2002).

Financial Peace Planner: A Step-by-Step Guide to Restoring Your Family's Financial Health, Dave Ramsey (Penguin Books, 1998).

For Richer, Not Poorer: The Money Book for Couples, Ruth L. Hayden (Health Communications, Inc., 1999).

The Frugal Senior: Hundreds of Creative Ways to Stretch a Dollar! (A Best Half of Life Book), Rich Gray (Quill Driver Books, 2005).

Get a Financial Life: Personal Finance in Your Twenties and Thirties, Beth Kobliner (Fireside, 2009).

Get Financially Naked: How to Talk Money with Your Honey, Manisha Thakor and Sharon Kedar (Adams Media, 2009).

Guide to Surviving Debt, Deanne Loonin (National Consumer Law Center, 2010).

How to Debt-Proof Your Marriage, Mary Hunt (Revell, 2008).

How to Get Out of Debt, Stay Out of Debt & Live Prosperously, Jerrold Mundis (Bantam Books, 2003). Based on the proven principles and techniques of Debtors Anonymous.

How to Wipe Out Your Student Loans and Be Debt Free Fast, Martha Maeda (Atlantic Publishing Company, 2009).

The Insider's Guide to Credit Repair, K. E. Varner (Career Press, 2008).

Invest in Yourself: Six Secrets to a Rich Life, Marc Eisenson, Gerri Detweiler, and Nancy Castleman (John Wiley and Sons, 2001).

I Shop, Therefore I Am: Compulsive Buying and the Search for Self, April Lane Benson (Jason Aronson, 2000).*

Kiplinger's Money Smart Women: Everything You Need to Know to Achieve a Lifetime of Financial Security, Janet Bodnar (Kaplan, 2006).

Making the Most of Your Money Now: The Classic Bestseller Completely Revised for the New Economy, Jane Bryant Quinn (Simon & Schuster, 2009).

Managing Your Money All-in-One For Dummies® (Wiley Publishing, 2009).

Miserly Moms: Living Well on Less in a Tough Economy, Jonni McCoy (Bethany House, 2009).

Money 911: Your Most Pressing Money Questions Answered, Your Money Emergencies Solved, Jean Chatzky (Harper, 2010).

Money Advice for Your Successful Remarriage: Handling Delicate Financial Issues with Love and Understanding, Patricia Schiff Estess (ASJA Press, 2001).

Money Drunk, Money Sober: 90 Days to Financial Freedom, Mark Bryan and Julia Cameron (Wellspring/Ballantine, 1999).

Money for Life: Budgeting Success and Financial Fitness in Just 12 Weeks, Steven B. Smith (In2M Corporation, 2007).

Money Habitudes—For Couples, Syble Solomon and Abby Donnelly (LifeWise Productions, 2005).

Money Harmony: Resolving Money Conflicts in Your Life and Relationships, Olivia Mellan (Walker & Company, 1995).

The Money-Saving Idea Book: Inside Tips for Starving Students, Frugal Seniors, and Every Financial Survivor, Ed Creager (CreateSpace, 2008).

---

*NOTE: Considering the issue and the price, I recommend you find a copy at the library or a used copy or visit *http://stoppingoverspending.com*.

The Motley Fool Personal Finance Workbook: A Foolproof Guide to Organizing Your Cash and Building Wealth, David Gardner, et al. (Fireside, 2002).

One-Income Household: How to Do a Lot with a Little, Susan Reynolds and Lauren Bakken (Adams Media, 2009).

Overcoming Overspending: A Winning Plan for Spenders and Their Partners, Olivia Mellan and Sherry Christie (Money Harmony Books, 2009).

Overcoming Underearning: Overcome Your Money Fears and Earn What You Deserve, Barbara Stanny (Harper Paperbacks, 2009).

Personal Finance For Dummies®, 6th ed., Eric Tyson (For Dummies, 2009).

Personal Finance Workbook For Dummies®, Sheryl Garrett, CFP (Wiley Publishing, 2008).

The Pocket Idiot's Guide to Living on a Budget, Peter J. Sander and Jennifer Basye Sander (Alpha Books, 2005).

Possum Living: How to Live Well Without a Job and With (Almost) No Money, Dolly Freed (Tin House Books, 2010).

The Power to Prosper: 21 Days to Financial Freedom, Michelle Singletory (Zondervan, 2010).

Prince Charming Isn't Coming: How Women Get Smart About Money, Barbara Stanny (Penguin, 2007).

Reduce Debt, Reduce Stress: Real Life Solutions for Solving Your Credit Crisis, Gerri Detweiler, Nancy Castleman, and Marc Eisenson (Good Advice Press Publications, 2009).

Rich Dad, Poor Dad: What the Rich Teach Their Kids About Money—That the Poor and the Middle Class Do Not, Robert T. Kiyosaki and Sharon L. Lechter (Business Plus, 2010).

Rich Dad Poor Dad for Teens: The Secrets About Money—That You Don't Learn in School!, Robert T. Kiyosaki and Sharon L. Lechter (Running Press Miniature Editions, 2009).

Richest Man in Babylon, George S. Clason (Classic House Books, 2008).

Secrets of the Millionaire Mind: Mastering the Inner Game of Wealth, T. Harv Eker (HarperCollins Publishers, 2005).

The Seven Stages of Money Maturity: Understanding the Spirit and Value of Money in Your Life, George Kinder (Dell, 2000).

Slash Your Debt: Save Money and Secure Your Future—Winning Debt Consolidation Strategies From America's Top Credit Experts, Gerri Detweiler, Marc Eisenson, and Nancy Castleman (Financial Literacy Center, 2006).

Smart Couples Finish Rich: 9 Steps to Creating a Rich Future for You and Your Partner, David Bach (Broadway, 2002).

Spent: Break the Buying Obsession and Discover Your True Worth, Sally Palaian (Hazelden Publishing, 2009).

Suze Orman's Action Plan: New Rules for New Times, Suze Orman (Spiegel & Grau, 2010).

To Buy or Not to Buy: Why We Overshop and How to Stop, April Lane Benson (Trumpeter Books, 2008).

The Total Money Makeover: A Proven Plan for Financial Fitness, Dave Ramsey (Thomas Nelson Publishers, 2009).

The Truth about Money, 4th ed., Ric Edelman (Harper, 2010).

Turning Your Debt Into Wealth: A Guide to Keeping More of the Money You Earn, Ron DuBois (CreateSpace, 2008).

The Ultimate Credit Handbook: How to Double Your Credit, Cut Your Debt, and Have a Lifetime of Great Credit, 3rd ed., Gerri Detweiler (Plume, 2003).

Your Money or Your Life: 9 Steps to Transforming Your Relationship with Money and Achieving Financial Independence; Revised and Updated for the 21st Century, by Vicki Robin, Joe Dominquez, and Monique Tilford (Penguin, 2008).

Zero Debt: The Ultimate Guide to Financial Freedom, Lynnette Khalfani-Cox (Advantage World Press, 2008).

Zero Debt for College Grads: From Student Loans to Financial Freedom, Lynette Khalfani (Kaplan Publishing, 2007).

Online Resources

Now, with such an abundance of online information, the real skill is using effective searching techniques for finding the most helpful information. The other skill is to be discerning about the accuracy, value, and security of the information and websites you do find and actually use.

Rather than spending endless hours doing a key word search on the major search engines, I recommend starting out with the websites listed in this section, which range from major corporation networks to homegrown common sense and a few blogs. They all have a phenomenal amount of valuable information and have a primary focus or informative section on general basic money management with topics covering, but not limited to, the following:

- Budgeting
- Credit
- Credit cards
- Debt
- Spending
- Spending guidelines
- Saving money
- Money attitudes
- Recovery issues

Many of these websites provide excellent articles, books, and online news-letters—often for free or discounted.

One topic not specifically included is "Children and Money," which is truly a topic of its own. Even though I did not include any of the valuable websites dedicated to this subject, the topic is still well covered in a number of the websites on this list. Be sure to do a search under the specific topic, and you will discover numerous websites designed for parents wanting to teach their children about money, as well as websites for kids that offer creative, hands-on experiences with banking, handling and tracking their allowance and gift money, and much more. Janet Bodnar, Editor at Kiplinger's magazine, is a prolific writer and author on the topic of children and money.

There are also now hundreds of convenient and well-designed calculators at various websites for developing basic budgets, calculating debt payoff or savings, and determining loan terms and total costs.

Other websites offer special debt management counseling and payment services. Be cautious as you explore these particular companies, even if they are listed as nonprofit. See "Getting Online Help for Debt" on page 110 for a review of what to expect from legitimate debt management services.

If this endless amount of information seems overwhelming, one way to narrow down your search efficiently is by going to the larger portals, which are all-inclusive sites. A few of these large services, like MSN, AOL, and Yahoo! are marked with asterisks **. The website address provided in the list below should take you directly to the personal finance section and save you a few layers of searching. If you do start on the home page, search around for the buttons, words, or tabs that indicate titles like "Money," "Budgets," "Personal Finance," "Family Finance," "Money 101," "Money Management," "Life and Money," "Planning," "Consumer Credit or Debt," and "Education" to get you started. You will often find a motherlode of articles archived by topic and/or author. Most of these articles are written and researched by some of the top financial authors and experts in the country.

Nearly every article and website you view will have a host of additional related links to keep your search moving.

For additional lists of online resources in this book, be sure to refer to the following sections:

Identity Theft—Online Resources and Fraud Hotlines—page 18
Online Financial Calculators—page 107
Getting Online Help for Debt—page 110
Opt-Out Resources—page 16

AARP
www.aarp.org/money

About.com (part of New York Times Company)
about.com/money

Almost Frugal—Learning About Frugality
http://almostfrugal.com

American Consumer Credit Counseling
www.consumercredit.com/index.html

AOL Money and Finance
www.walletpop.com

Ask the Advisor—Top 100 Personal Finance Blogs
www.yourcreditadvisor.com/blog/2007/02/top_100_persona.html

Bankrate.com—Independent Financial Information
www.bankrate.com/life-money.aspx

Better Budgeting
www.betterbudgeting.com

Board of Governors of the Federal Reserve System
http://federalreserve.gov/consumerinfo/personalfinance.htm

Card Ratings
www.cardratings.com

Checking Finder
www.checkingfinder.com

Choose to Save Education Program
www.choosetosave.org

**CNN Money
http://money.cnn.com/pf/

Consumer Credit Counseling Services
www.cccsintl.org

Consumer Reports
www.consumerreports.org

Coupons
www.coupons.com

Credit.com
www.credit.com

Credit Education
www.crediteducation.org

Daily Finance
www.dailyfinance.com

Dave Ramsey
www.daveramsey.com

Debit Facts
http://debitfacts.org

Debtors Anonymous—12 Step
www.debtorsanonymous.com

Dolans.com—Money Made Simple
www.dolans.com

The Dollar Stretcher: Living Better for Less
www.stretcher.com

Family Resource Center
www.ourfamilyplace.com

Federal Consumer Information Center
www.pueblo.gsa.gov

Financial Planning: Complete Guide to Personal Finance and Financial Success
www.financialplan.about.com

Finish Rich Resource Center
www.finishrich.com/free_resources/fr_lattefactor.php

**Fox News
www.foxbusiness.com/personal-finance/index.html

Get Rich Slowly
www.getrichslowly.org/blog

Good Advice Press
www.goodadvicepress.com

Institute of Consumer Financial Education
www.financial-education-icfe.org

Jump $tart Coalition for Personal Financial Literacy
www.jumpstart.org

Kiplinger Magazine Online
www.kiplinger.com/family-finance

Mary Hunt's Debt Proof Living
www.debtproofliving.com

Miserly Moms
www.miserlymoms.com

Money Habitudes (money management card game)
www.moneyhabitudes.com

Money Saving Ideas—Gail Vaz-Oxlade
www.money-saving-ideas.net/money-jar.html

**MSN Money
moneycentral.msn.com/personal-finance

My Money (collaborative site of 20 U.S. government agencies)
www.mymoney.gov

National Association of Consumer Bankruptcy Attorneys
http://nacba.org

National Association of Personal Financial Advisors
www.napfa.org

National Consumer Law Center
www.nclc.org

National Foundation for Consumer Credit
www.nfcc.org

NOLO—Legal Solutions for You, Your Family & Your Business
www.nolo.com (click on Personal Finance and Retirement)

Oprah.com
www.oprah.com/money.html

Short Cut$—Real Savings, Real Simple
http://shortcuts.com

The Simple Dollar—Financial Talk for the Rest of Us
www.thesimpledollar.com

Smart About Money—National Endowment for Financial Education
http://smartaboutmoney.org

Smart Money
www.smartmoney.com/pf/?nav=dropTab

Stopping Overshopping
http://stoppingovershopping.com

Top Ten Reviews—We Do the Research So You Don't Have To
www.toptenreviews.com

U.S. Financial Literacy & Education Commission
http://mymoney.gov

**USA Today
www.usatoday.com/money/default.htm

Women's Institute for Financial Education
www.wife.org

**Yahoo! Finance Education Center Managing Debt
http://finance.yahoo.com/personal-finance
http://biz.yahoo.com/edu/ed_debt.html

YOUNG MONEY Magazine
www.youngmoney.com

Index

About the Author

JUDY LAWRENCE, **MS, Ed**, is a financial counselor and popular speaker and workshop facilitator on basic money management. She has been a featured guest on numerous television and radio shows throughout the country and has been quoted in a variety of publications for over three decades. *The Budget Kit* was originally developed in 1981 as *Common Cent$: The Complete Money Management Workbook* and was a true pioneer in the early days of limited personal financial management books.

As a result of her various experiences, such as being a REALTOR®, college rep, and counselor at a boarding school on the Navajo Reservation and a large technical college, Judy saw the need for a nonintimidating workbook that could immediately be used by people with limited time or limited organizing and budgeting skills. Her foresight during the "low-tech" era of the early 1980s is just as timely now in this high-tech information-age 21st century.

She launched a unique financial budget counseling practice in the 80s in Albuquerque, New Mexico, where she counseled couples, individuals, and small businesses, and later expanded her business to become a family law court-appointed expert developing and evaluating personal budgets. Her techniques and workbooks, including *The Money Tracker, The Family Memory Book,* and *Magic, Miracles, and Synchronicity Gratitude Journal,* have all focused on providing valuable information and basic, encouraging, and extremely user-friendly support.

After living in Cupertino, California, for ten years and experiencing life in the heart of the Silicon Valley during the first decade of the new millennium, Judy now lives again in Albuquerque, New Mexico, and continues to serve clients through her national consulting practice for financial counseling by phone and email. She also enjoys her new involvement with the Collaborative Practice Group, participating as a professional team member with collaborative divorces.

You can visit Judy's website at *www.moneytracker.com* or arrange directly for media interviews, speaking engagements, or telephone consultations by calling 505-554-2638 or 408-529-6474 or by emailing *judy@moneytracker.com*.

ATTENTION MS EXCEL USERS

As a value-added service, it is now possible to combine the simplicity of the traditional manual worksheet with the technology of immediate calculations. Available in the exact same format as the workbook are the four worksheets with the most calculations: the Monthly Expense Record, the Monthly Budget Worksheet, the Yearly Budget Worksheet, and the Debt Payoff Record. All totals are calculated automatically, saving you hours of manual calculator time. Currently there is a small fee. For more information, visit *http://moneytracker.com/books-TheBudgetKitExcel.htm*.